Spelling Workbook

Siegfried Engelmann

mheducation.com/prek-12

Copyright © 2021 McGraw-Hill Education

All rights reserved. No part of this publication may be reproduced or distributed in any form or by any means, or stored in a database or retrieval system, without the prior written consent of McGraw-Hill Education, including, but not limited to, network storage or transmission, or broadcast for distance learning.

Send all inquiries to:
McGraw-Hill Education
8787 Orion Place
Columbus, OH 43240

ISBN: 978-0-07-905374-9
MHID: 0-07-905374-2

Printed in the United States of America.

3 4 5 6 7 8 9 LMN 25 24 23 22

Name _____

A

wander   listen   search   build   view   sort

B

1. ____ ring
2. ____ viewing
3. ____ listen
4. ____ listening
5. ____ rebuild
6. ____ searching

C

1. _____
2. _____
3. _____
4. _____
5. _____
6. _____

D Each sentence has one misspelled word. Write each word correctly on the blank.

1. She serched the cloudless, starry sky.   _____

2. Which would be the nicer choise, swimming or packing?   _____

END OF LESSON 1

A

equal   cheap   straight   light   sleep   quote

B

1. _ _ _ t e n
2. _ _ _ _
3. _ u _ _ _
4. _ a _ _ e _
5. _ i _ w
6. _ e a _ _ _

C

1. _____
2. _____
3. _____
4. _____
5. _____
6. _____

D Each sentence has one misspelled word. Write each word correctly on the blank.

1. He was <u>helpfull</u> at <u>watering</u> the <u>lawn</u>.   _____

2. Could you make a <u>copy</u> of this <u>sine</u> for me?   _____

3. We were <u>happy</u> with the new <u>reserch</u> building.   _____

END OF LESSON 2

Name _____

A

spell   source   stretch   child   care   cloud

B

n   i   a   p   m   e   b   o   h   r   u   f

C

1. __ __ __ __ i __ h t
2. __ u __ __ e
3. __ __ __ t __ __
4. __ __ __ a l
5. __ __ g __ __
6. __ __ a __ __ __

D

1. _____   4. _____

2. _____   5. _____

3. _____   6. _____

Lesson 3

E **Each sentence has one misspelled word. Write each word correctly on the blank.**

1. It was foolish to think the rental car would be falltless. _____

2. We can enjoy this deliteful swimming pool. _____

3. She waited hopefully for the note to arrive hear. _____

END OF LESSON 3

Name _____ **4**

A

happy   lock   study   glory   sign   people

B

1. __ __ __ __ t __ __
2. __ __ __ __ i __ h __
3. __ __ __ __ __
4. __ __ u __ c __
5. __ __ __ __ __
6. __ __ o __ l __

C

1. _____ + _____ = wandering
2. _____ + _____ = childless
3. _____ + _____ = misquote
4. _____ + _____ = unhappy
5. _____ + _____ = cheapest
6. _____ + _____ = resource

D Make a small <u>v</u> above every vowel letter.
Make a small <u>c</u> above every consonant letter.

n e f i o m e i h

d a p t c u b o h

E Cross out the misspelled words in these sentences.
Then write the words correctly above the crossed-out words.

Did you lissen to the kwote?

He did not wandor in a straite line.

Lesson 5 is a test lesson. There is no worksheet.

Name

A

quiet   fight   break   port   school   author

B

1. _____   4. _____

2. _____   5. _____

3. _____   6. _____

C

1. quote + ing = _____

2. care + less = _____

3. ripe + est = _____

4. like + ness = _____

5. stage + ing = _____

6. fine + est = _____

7. choke + ing = _____

8. sore + ness = _____

Lesson 6

D Fill in the blanks to show the morphographs in each word.

1. _____ + _____ = stretching

2. _____ + _____ = cheapest

3. _____ + _____ + _____ = rebuilding

4. _____ + _____ = darkness

5. _____ + _____ = careless

6. _____ + _____ = unhappy

E Cross out the misspelled words in these sentences.
Then write the words correctly above the crossed-out words.

I made a careles mistake.

Some peeple sleap better than others.

END OF LESSON 6

Lesson 6

Name _____

7

A

caught   picture   together   wrong

B

Please answer the question.

_____

_____

C

1. __ u __ __ o __
2. __ __ __ e __
3. __ __ e __ __

4. __ __ o __ l __
5. __ __ h __ __ __
6. __ __ __ __ i g __ __

D

1. like + able   =   _____
2. fine + est   =   _____
3. ripe + ness   =   _____
4. hope + less   =   _____
5. stage + ing   =   _____
6. cure + able   =   _____

Lesson 7

E Fill in the blanks to show the morphographs in each word.

1. _____ + _____ = portable
2. _____ + _____ + _____ = remarkable
3. _____ + _____ = uneven
4. _____ + _____ = quietest
5. _____ + _____ + _____ = sleeplessness
6. _____ + _____ + _____ = unbreakable
7. _____ + _____ = searching
8. _____ + _____ = boldness

END OF LESSON 7

Name _____

A

might　　　　story　　　　style　　　　voice　　　　choice

B

1. win
2. sharp
3. shop
4. farm
5. mad
6. grab
7. star
8. port

C

_ _ e a s _　_ _ _ w e _　_ _ _

_ _ _ s t _ _ .

_____

D Add the morphographs together.
Some of the words follow the rule about dropping the final e.

1. write + ing   = _____
2. use + able   = _____
3. straight + est = _____
4. shine + ing   = _____
5. like + ness   = _____
6. use + less   = _____
7. dark + ness   = _____
8. large + est   = _____

Lesson 8

E Fill in the blanks to show the morphographs in each word.

1. _____ + _____ = stretched

2. _____ + _____ + _____ = thoughtlessness

3. _____ + _____ + _____ = repainted

4. _____ + _____ = stretchable

5. _____ + _____ = mistake

6. _____ + _____ + _____ = unwashable

7. _____ + _____ + _____ = helplessness

8. _____ + _____ = clouded

F Each sentence has one misspelled word. Write each word correctly on the blank.

1. The playful, old farmer still has a boyischness to him.   _____

2. The golden sun has nearly rissen.   _____

3. As Amy was skiping here, she slipped and fell.   _____

END OF LESSON 8

Name _____

9

A

thought   world   serve   grudge   charge

B

_ _ _ _ _   _ _ _ _ _   _ _ _

_ _ _ _ _ _ .

_____

C

1. slip   3. win   5. flat   7. part

2. leak   4. norm   6. drip   8. snug

D

1. _____   4. _____

2. _____   5. _____

3. _____   6. _____

Lesson 9   13

E **Add the morphographs together.**
Some of the words follow the rule about dropping the final e.

1. nice + er = _____

2. pre + serve + ing = _____

3. ripe + ness = _____

4. charge + ing = _____

5. time + less = _____

6. love + able = _____

Lesson 10 is a test lesson. There is no worksheet.

Name _____

A

busy   sailboat   noise   sketch   twice

B

1. _____
2. _____

C

Double c when cvc + v

1. run + er   = _____
2. author + ing = _____
3. sad + ly   = _____
4. sad + est   = _____
5. swim + ing = _____
6. mad + ly   = _____
7. stop + ed   = _____
8. farm + er   = _____

Lesson 11

D

1. __ __ __ u __ __ __
2. __ __ y __ __
3. __ __ __ __ __ e
4. __ e __ __ __
5. __ __ __ __ i __ __ __
6. __ u __ __ o __

E

Add the morphographs together.
Some of the words follow the rule about dropping the final e.

1. quote + able = _____

2. de + fine + ed = _____

3. use + less = _____

4. mis + shape + ed = _____

5. serve + ing = _____

6. wide + ly = _____

7. time + less = _____

8. hope + less + ly = _____

END OF LESSON 11

Name _____

A

bench   chalk   person   several   through

B

1. _____ 4. _____

2. _____ 5. _____

3. _____ 6. _____

C

1. star + ed   = _____

2. flop + ing = _____

3. run + ing   = _____

4. mad + ness = _____

5. drag + ing = _____

6. water + ing = _____

7. big + est   = _____

8. fit + ness = _____

D Add the morphographs together.
Some of the words follow the rule about dropping the final e.

1. cure + able = _____
2. wide + est = _____
3. re + place + ed = _____
4. use + able = _____
5. un + like + ly = _____
6. care + less = _____

E Fill in the blanks to show the morphographs in each word.

1. _____ + _____ + _____ = thoughtlessly
2. _____ + _____ = lighten
3. _____ + _____ + _____ = departed
4. _____ + _____ = straighten
5. _____ + _____ + _____ = delightful
6. _____ + _____ + _____ = unequally

F Each sentence has one misspelled word.
Write each word correctly on the blank.

1. Be sure to study the rite spelling words. _____
2. Reveiw the research, and then write the paper. _____
3. Ann was not happy to see the missquote _____
   on her sign.

END OF LESSON 12

Name _____ | 13

A

wreck   note   different   prove

B

1. __ __ __ o u __ __   4. __ __ __ l __
2. __ __ __ e __ a __   5. __ __ __ __ o __
3. __ k __ __ __ __

C

cvc + v

1. stop + ing = _____
2. wrap + er   = _____
3. fit + ness = _____
4. mad + est   = _____
5. sad + ly   = _____
6. bliss + ful = _____
7. spot + ed   = _____
8. big + est   = _____

D

1. _____ + _____ = hoping
2. _____ + _____ = finest
3. _____ + _____ = worthless
4. _____ + _____ = likable
5. _____ + _____ = useless
6. _____ + _____ = package
7. _____ + _____ = purest
8. _____ + _____ = staging

E Draw a line from each word to its clue.

1. clothes •   • Can you ▆▆▆ the music?
2. here •   • put words on paper
3. feat •   • what you wear
4. write •   • in this place
5. feet •   • correct
6. hear •   • His boots keep his ▆▆▆ warm.
7. close •   • Please ▆▆▆ the door when you leave.
8. right •   • an act of great skill

F Each sentence has one misspelled word. Write each word correctly on the blank.

1. Search for the sorce of that quote. _____

2. The child went to sleep under a cloudles sky. _____

3. Don't worry about wrecking it as you unrap it. _____

END OF LESSON 13

14

Name _____

A

speak   pinch   pure

B

1. _____
   _____

2. _____
   _____

C

1. _____ + _____ = _____
2. _____ + _____ = _____
3. _____ + _____ = _____
4. _____ + _____ = _____
5. _____ + _____ = _____
6. _____ + _____ = _____

D Fill in the blanks to show the morphographs in each word.

1. _____ + _____ = formal
2. _____ + _____ = package
3. _____ + _____ = thoughtful
4. _____ + _____ = quietly
5. _____ + _____ + _____ = helpfully
6. _____ + _____ = portable
7. _____ + _____ = useless
8. _____ + _____ + _____ = thoughtlessness

E Add the morphographs together.
Some of the words follow the rule about dropping the final e.

1. fine + al = _____
2. note + able = _____
3. re + fine + ed = _____
4. un + prove + en = _____
5. serve + ing = _____
6. hope + less + ness = _____
7. charge + ing = _____
8. re + source + ful = _____

Lesson 14

F Each sentence has one misspelled word. Write each word correctly on the blank.

1. Please keep searching until you find the rippest apple. _____

2. The author had to ansser six questions. _____

3. The child seems to hold a gruge against me. _____

Lesson 15 is a test lesson. There is no worksheet.

A

1. w __ __ __ __
2. __ __ __ __ e __ e __ __
3. __ e __ __ __ __
4. __ __ __ __ u __ __
5. __ __ __ a __
6. __ __ __ e __ a __

B

1. _____   4. _____
2. _____   5. _____
3. _____   6. _____

C

Add the morphographs together.
Some of the words follow the rule about doubling the final c in short words.

1. spin + ing   = _____
2. fool + ish   = _____
3. wrap + er   = _____
4. rent + al   = _____
5. sad + ness   = _____
6. norm + al   = _____
7. drip + ed   = _____
8. grab + ed   = _____

D Circle the misspelled word in each group. Then write it correctly on the line.

1. person
   noize
   quiet
   school
   _____

2. bench
   light
   child
   sevral
   _____

3. scetch
   break
   author
   picture
   _____

4. twise
   chalk
   prove
   style
   _____

5. choice
   straght
   might
   equal
   _____

6. chardge
   happy
   stretch
   sleep
   _____

E Each sentence has one misspelled word. Write each word correctly on the blank.

1. She has a remarckable style of writing.   _____

2. Was it wrong to voice what I thougt?   _____

3. I was careless with my speling and made a mistake.   _____

END OF LESSON 16

Name _____

A

1. happy
2. boy
3. you
4. yellow
5. berry
6. sturdy
7. play

B

1. _____
2. _____
3. _____
4. _____
5. _____
6. _____

C

D

1. _____ + _____ = shopper
2. _____ + _____ = running
3. _____ + _____ = fitness
4. _____ + _____ = stopped
5. _____ + _____ = planning
6. _____ + _____ = swimmer

E

Add the morphographs together. The morphograph u is a vowel letter.

1. shine + y = _____
2. cloud + y = _____
3. self + ish + ly = _____
4. gum + y = _____
5. store + age = _____
6. rose + y = _____
7. tribe + al = _____
8. chop + y = _____

F

Each sentence has one misspelled word. Write each word correctly on the blank.

1. School might seem unnending by the spring. _____

2. Please take a pitcher of us standing together. _____

3. It helped to prevue the story. _____

END OF LESSON 17

Name _____

A

length   strength   skate   sturdy   carry   fancy   value

B

1. _____   4. _____
2. _____   5. _____
3. _____   6. _____

C

1. _____   4. _____
2. _____   5. _____
3. _____   6. _____

D Add the morphographs together.
The morphograph <u>y</u> is a vowel letter.

1. fur + y   = _____
2. wire + y = _____
3. frost + y = _____
4. pup + y   = _____
5. stone + y = _____
6. dress + y = _____

Lesson 18

E Fill in the blanks to show the morphographs in each word.

1. _____ + _____ = sleepy
2. _____ + _____ = hoping
3. _____ + _____ + _____ = presented
4. _____ + _____ = saddest
5. _____ + _____ = warmest
6. _____ + _____ + _____ = selfishness
7. _____ + _____ + _____ = carelessly
8. _____ + _____ = starring

F Each sentence has one misspelled word. Write each word correctly on the blank.

1. After rebiulding the school, the workers repainted it. _____

2. It was remarkable how brightly the sun was shineing. _____

3. The farmer grew the largest and finnest pumpkins. _____

END OF LESSON 18

Name _____

A

1. __ __ __ __ n g __ __   4. __ u __ __ __
2. __ __ __ __ __ __ e __ __ 5. __ __ u __ __ __
3. __ __ __ __ __   6. __ e __ __ __

B Fill in the blanks to show the morphographs in each word.

1. _____ + _____ + _____ = preserved
2. _____ + _____ = strengthen
3. _____ + _____ = global
4. _____ + _____ = personal
5. _____ + _____ = usage
6. _____ + _____ = biggest
7. _____ + _____ + _____ = misspelling
8. _____ + _____ = valuable

C Cross out the misspelled words in these sentences.
Then write the words correctly above the crossed-out words.

Draw a strate line throuh each mispelling.

A buzy auther came to our skool.

Lesson 19

D These words are in the word search.
Circle 7 or more of the words.

research	hopeless
childish	author
happy	dark
care	light
answer	quote
wander	right

```
c  r  e  s  e  a  r  c  h
h  a  p  p  y  n  h  q  o
i  w  r  r  y  s  a  q  p
l  r  a  e  e  w  u  u  e
d  i  i  n  r  e  t  o  l
i  a  g  g  d  r  h  t  e
s  a  r  h  h  e  o  e  s
h  o  r  k  t  t  r  e  s
```

E Each sentence has one misspelled word. Write each word correctly on the blank.

1. Tom was busy authering his biggest book.   _____

2. It is blissful to sit on this bench on such a deliteful day.   _____

3. Use the chalk to darcken and define your picture.   _____

Lesson 20 is a test lesson. There is no worksheet.

Name _____

21

A

1. _____ 4. _____
2. _____ 5. _____
3. _____ 6. _____

B

1. _____
2. _____

C

_____
_____
_____
_____
_____
_____
_____
_____
_____

D **Add the morphographs together. Remember to use your spelling rules.**

1. state + ly = _____
2. step + ing = _____
3. spot + less = _____
4. safe + ly = _____
5. style + ish = _____
6. store + age = _____
7. de + serve + ed = _____
8. re + fine + ed = _____
9. win + er = _____
10. un + plan + ed = _____
11. big + est = _____
12. prove + ing = _____
13. pure + ly = _____
14. skate + ing = _____

E **Each sentence has one misspelled word. Write each word correctly on the blank.**

1. The <u>rental</u> <u>saleboat</u> was a <u>wreck</u>. _____
2. It is <u>unlikley</u> they will get <u>through</u> the <u>fitness</u> test. _____
3. I can <u>prove</u> <u>there</u> was a note on the <u>pakkage</u>. _____

END OF LESSON 21

Name _____

A

1. _____
2. _____

B Add the morphographs together.

1. late + ly   = _____
2. grace + ful   = _____
3. real + ly   = _____
4. fault + less   = _____
5. fire + ed   = _____
6. mis + judge   = _____
7. equal + ly   = _____
8. teach + er   = _____

C Circle each short word that ends cvc.
Remember: Short words have four letters or fewer.
The letter **y** is a vowel letter at the end of a morphograph.

1. trip
2. joy
3. wander
4. step
5. fury
6. pray
7. drop
8. swim
9. pass
10. shop
11. tray
12. hit

Lesson 22

D Cross out the misspelled words in these sentences.
Then write the words correctly above the crossed-out words.

I like to wandor thrugh the woulds.

The speeker missquoted his sorce.

E These words are in the word search.
Circle 7 or more of the words.

strength	hate	rent
stretch	rest	best
swim	mash	wash
sack	hot	catch

s	h	o	t	m	s	b	c
s	t	r	c	h	a	e	h
w	a	r	e	s	t	s	t
s	t	r	e	n	g	t	h
w	a	s	h	t	t	s	a
i	i	c	a	t	c	h	t
m	m	i	k	s	s	h	e

F Each sentence has one misspelled word.
Write each word correctly on the blank.

1. The runner thougtlessly jogged through the roses. _____

2. She stoppd twice in the swimming race. _____

3. Mike replaced the mishaped hat with a different one. _____

END OF LESSON 22

36 Lesson 22

Name _____

A

1. _____   4. _____
2. _____   5. _____
3. _____

B

1. _____   6. _____
2. _____   7. _____
3. _____   8. _____
4. _____   9. _____
5. _____   10. _____

C Draw a line from each word to its clue.

1. vary • • We'll fill the ▢ with dirt.
2. whole • • correct
3. hear • • change something
4. hole • • put words on paper
5. here • • Keep your shoes on your ▢.
6. write • • They left their coats ▢.
7. close • • Have you read the ▢ book?
8. feet • • what you wear
9. right • • I don't ▢ any noise.
10. clothes • • Please ▢ the door.

Lesson 23   37

D Fill in the blanks to show the morphographs in each word.

1. _____ + _____ + _____ = carefully
2. _____ + _____ + _____ = rebuilding
3. _____ + _____ = storage
4. _____ + _____ + _____ = related
5. _____ + _____ + _____ = delightful
6. _____ + _____ = lengthy
7. _____ + _____ + _____ = restlessness
8. _____ + _____ = wrapper
9. _____ + _____ + _____ = wonderfully
10. _____ + _____ + _____ = preserved

E Each sentence has one misspelled word. Write each word correctly on the blank.

1. They will be <u>serving</u> <u>several</u> foods at the <u>formel</u> dinner. _____

2. They were <u>helpfull</u> at <u>fixing</u> the <u>rental</u> car. _____

3. The <u>final</u> <u>passage</u> was the <u>sadest</u> in the book. _____

END OF LESSON 23

Name _____

A

1. _____
2. _____

B

1. _____ 4. _____
2. _____ 5. _____
3. _____ 6. _____

C Make 11 real words from the morphographs in the box.

| ed | er | rent | bare | ing | serve | dine |

1. _____ 7. _____
2. _____ 8. _____
3. _____ 9. _____
4. _____ 10. _____
5. _____ 11. _____
6. _____

Lesson 24

D Fill in the blanks to show the morphographs in each word.

1. _____ + _____ = shopping

2. _____ + _____ = widely

3. _____ + _____ = hopeless

4. _____ + _____ = hoping

5. _____ + _____ = runner

6. _____ + _____ = cared

Lesson 25 is a test lesson. There is no worksheet.

Name _____

26

A

consonant-y + anything except i

1. study + ed = _____
2. happy + ness = _____
3. play + er = _____
4. copy + ed = _____
5. pity + ful = _____
6. deny + ed = _____

B

1. _____   5. _____
2. _____   6. _____
3. _____   7. _____
4. _____   8. _____

C Each sentence has one misspelled word. Write each word correctly on the blank.

1. Is it normel to skate on a rainy day?   _____
2. On a sunny day, a heavy coat is uneeded.   _____
3. I felt foolish in my fancey, shiny dress.   _____

Lesson 26   41

D Make 15 real words from the morphographs in the box.

| hope | use | ful | less | ly | care | rest |

1. _____
2. _____
3. _____
4. _____
5. _____
6. _____
7. _____
8. _____
9. _____
10. _____
11. _____
12. _____
13. _____
14. _____
15. _____

E Add the morphographs together.
Some of the words follow the rule about doubling the final <u>c</u> in short words.

1. big + est = _____
2. shop + ing = _____
3. sad + en = _____
4. deal + er = _____
5. run + ing = _____
6. mad + ness = _____
7. strength + en = _____
8. form + al + ly = _____

END OF LESSON 26

Name _____

27

A

1. _____ 4. _____
2. _____ 5. _____
3. _____ 6. _____

B

consonant-y + anything except i

1. sturdy + ness = _____
2. fury + ous   = _____
3. worry + ed   = _____
4. fancy + ful   = _____
5. play + ful   = _____
6. hurry + ed   = _____

C

Lesson 27 43

D Add the morphographs together.

1. style + ish = _____
2. store + age = _____
3. fine + al + ly = _____
4. re + mark + able = _____
5. un + pre + serve + ed = _____
6. mis + take + en = _____
7. de + light + ed = _____
8. gold + en = _____
9. harm + less + ly = _____
10. pre + view + ed = _____
11. quiet + est = _____
12. noise + y = _____
13. pre + date + ed = _____
14. sad + en = _____

E Each sentence has one misspelled word. Write each word correctly on the blank.

1. The sleepy puppy had wirey hair. _____
2. I pulled the fury dog out of the hole. _____
3. She presented the swimmer with a shiney medal. _____

END OF LESSON 27

Name _____

A

tax   box   fox

B

1. _____
2. _____

C Write <u>s</u> or <u>es</u> in the second column.
Then add the morphographs together.

s or **es**

1. press + _____ = _____
2. shop + _____ = _____
3. dish + _____ = _____
4. stretch + _____ = _____
5. goat + _____ = _____
6. glass + _____ = _____

D Each sentence has one misspelled word.
Write each word correctly on the blank.

1. Danny <u>carelessly</u> <u>dripped</u> ink on the _____
   <u>goldin</u> fabric.

2. <u>Finely</u> <u>preserved</u> items are the most <u>valueable</u>. _____

3. You can <u>strengthen</u> your <u>hole</u> paper by _____
   correcting any <u>misspelled</u> words.

Lesson 28 **45**

E Add the morphographs together.
Some of the words follow the rule about changing **y** to **i**.

consonant-y + anything except i

1. copy + er = _____
2. sturdy + est = _____
3. cry + er = _____
4. dry + ed = _____
5. stay + ed = _____
6. sturdy + ness = _____

F Fill in the blanks to show the morphographs in each word.

1. _____ + _____ + _____ = informal
2. _____ + _____ = disease
3. _____ + _____ = easy
4. _____ + _____ = dropping
5. _____ + _____ = package
6. _____ + _____ + _____ = formally
7. _____ + _____ = hopeless
8. _____ + _____ = hoping

END OF LESSON 28

Name _____

A

1. pity + ful = _____

2. carry + ed = _____

3. fancy + est = _____

4. like + ly + est = _____

5. try + ing = _____

6. friend + ly + ness = _____

7. study + ing = _____

8. play + ful = _____

B

1. _____   6. _____

2. _____   7. _____

3. _____   8. _____

4. _____   9. _____

5. _____   10. _____

C

_____
_____
_____
_____
_____
_____
_____
_____

D Write s or es in the second column. Then add the morphographs together.

                      s or es

1. match + _____ = _____
2. tail + _____ = _____
3. pinch + _____ = _____
4. mess + _____ = _____
5. lunch + _____ = _____
6. glass + _____ = _____
7. farm + _____ = _____
8. bush + _____ = _____

E Each sentence has one misspelled word. Write each word correctly on the blank.

1. Our teacher deserved to be the winer. _____

2. They proved that the desiner was copying others. _____

3. The goat was wunderfully funny. _____

Lesson 30 is a test lesson. There is no worksheet.

31 Name _____

A Add the morphographs together.
Follow the rule for changing u to i.

1. happy + ness   = _____
2. stay + ed   = _____
3. try + ed   = _____
4. dry + ing   = _____
5. deny + al   = _____
6. hurry + ed   = _____
7. vary + ed   = _____
8. un + like + ly + ness = _____

B Make 14 real words from the morphographs in the box.

| de | er | fine | serve | light | ing | grade |

1. _____   8. _____
2. _____   9. _____
3. _____   10. _____
4. _____   11. _____
5. _____   12. _____
6. _____   13. _____
7. _____   14. _____

C Draw a line from each word to its clue.

1. whole • • That door has a ▮ in it.
2. vary • • Would you come ▮, please?
3. here • • They wrote a ▮ book.
4. hole • • what you wear
5. clothes • • change
6. very • • The play made me feel ▮ sad.

D Add the morphographs together.

1. con + strict = _____
2. re + in + state = _____
3. stitch + es = _____
4. worth + y = _____
5. store + age = _____
6. child + ish + ly = _____
7. luck + y = _____
8. con + form + ing = _____
9. fine + al + ly = _____
10. in + human = _____

END OF LESSON 31

32 Name _____

A

leave　　　neat　　　main　　　claim　　　children

B

Whose turn is it to move?

_____

C Add the morphographs together.
Some of the words follow the rule about changing y to i.

1. vary + ed = _____
2. happy + est = _____
3. spray + ed = _____
4. friend + ly + ness = _____
5. worry + ing = _____
6. carry + ed = _____

D Each sentence has one misspelled word. Write each word correctly on the blank.

1. We can't safely sail in such a pityful boat.　_____

2. The lenthy shopping trip was unplanned.　_____

3. Lately we have been dinning at really nice places.　_____

E. Write s or es in the second column. Then add the morphographs together.

                s or es

1. bench + _____ = _____
2. reach + _____ = _____
3. box + _____ = _____
4. wash + _____ = _____
5. claim + _____ = _____
6. mess + _____ = _____

F. Circle the misspelled word in each group. Then write it correctly on the line.

1. world
   cought
   shining
   wander

   _____

2. happy
   motor
   auther
   friend

   _____

3. stretch
   choice
   herb
   larje

   _____

4. equil
   change
   hopeful
   trace

   _____

5. depressing
   quiut
   human
   wrong

   _____

6. should
   would
   could
   noize

   _____

END OF LESSON 32

Lesson 32   53

33 Name _____

A

1. _____   7. _____
2. _____   8. _____
3. _____   9. _____
4. _____   10. _____
5. _____   11. _____
6. _____   12. _____

B

W h o s e _ u r _ _ _ _ _
_ _ _ o _ e ?

_____

C Each sentence has one misspelled word. Write each word correctly on the blank.

1. We were <u>hopeful</u> that our parade <u>flote</u> would be the <u>winner</u>.   _____

2. Our <u>server</u> at the <u>dinner</u> is <u>realated</u> to me.   _____

3. The <u>nice</u> girl <u>dezerved</u> a raise because she <u>cared</u> well for the plants.   _____

Lesson 33

D Fill in the blanks to show the morphographs in each word.

1. _____ + _____ = civilly
2. _____ + _____ + _____ = strengthening
3. _____ + _____ + _____ = informer
4. _____ + _____ = really
5. _____ + _____ = planning
6. _____ + _____ = changing
7. _____ + _____ + _____ = formally
8. _____ + _____ = wreckage
9. _____ + _____ + _____ = preplanned
10. _____ + _____ + _____ = hopefully

Lesson 33

E Add the morphographs together.
Some of the words follow the rule about changing u to i.

1. happy + ly = _____
2. con + fine = _____
3. in + side = _____
4. girl + ish + ness = _____
5. pity + ed = _____
6. un + claim + ed = _____
7. neat + ly = _____
8. like + ly + ness = _____
9. rain + y = _____
10. store + age = _____
11. norm + al + ly = _____
12. un + drink + able = _____
13. play + ful = _____
14. de + press + ing = _____
15. worry + ed = _____

END OF LESSON 33

Name _____

A

__ __ __ s e __ u __ __ __ __ __ __ __ __
__ o __ __ ?

_____

B

1. _____ + _____ = _____
2. _____ + _____ = _____
3. _____ + _____ = _____
4. _____ + _____ = _____
5. _____ + _____ = _____
6. _____ + _____ = _____

C

1. _____
2. _____

D Draw a line from each word to its clue.

1. lone • • change
2. vary • • put words on paper
3. write • • I can ▨ the music.
4. close • • by yourself
5. hear • • all parts together
6. whole • • Don't ▨ the window yet.

E Write s or es in the second column.
Then add the morphographs together.

                  s or es

1. patch + _____ = _____
2. box + _____ = _____
3. claim + _____ = _____
4. class + _____ = _____
5. reach + _____ = _____
6. sign + _____ = _____
7. match + _____ = _____
8. speech + _____ = _____

F **Each sentence has one misspelled word. Write each word correctly on the blank.**

1. She carryed the box with both arms. _____

2. John is careful as he brushs the coats of the animals. _____

3. Was it eazy to design the glasses? _____

Lesson 35 is a test lesson. There is no worksheet.

36 Name _____

A

1. _____ 4. _____
2. _____ 5. _____
3. _____ 6. _____

B

1. _____
2. _____

C Figure out the rule, and write it. Remember to spell the words correctly.

and the next morphograph begins with **v** . . . when the word ends **cvc** . . . Double the final **c** in a short word

_____

_____

D Each sentence has one misspelled word. Write each word correctly on the blank.

1. After <u>dropping</u> several items, the <u>dealer</u> <u>finaly</u> gave up. _____

2. I <u>hurryed</u> to finish <u>drying</u> the dishes. _____

3. <u>Hopefully</u> <u>you'll</u> search for <u>hapiness</u>. _____

E Fill in the blanks to show the morphographs in each word.

1. _____ + _____ = cloudy
2. _____ + _____ = valuable
3. _____ + _____ = equally
4. _____ + _____ = maddest
5. _____ + _____ + _____ = reinstate
6. _____ + _____ + _____ = informer
7. _____ + _____ + _____ = preserved
8. _____ + _____ + _____ = uselessly

F Circle the misspelled word in each group. Then write it correctly on the line.

1. brother
   story
   shuld
   were
   _____

2. rong
   wrap
   fancy
   civil
   _____

3. shineing
   hurried
   joyful
   wander
   _____

4. stretch
   civilly
   realy
   unfilling
   _____

5. swimer
   runner
   story
   restful
   _____

6. stretcher
   friendly
   unarmmed
   shopper
   _____

END OF LESSON 36

37

Name _____

A

1. __ __ __ i __
2. __ __ __ __ __ g h __
3. __ __ i __ __ __ __
4. __ r __ __ __ a __ __
5. __ __ __ i __ __
6. __ __ o __ __

B

1. _____   4. _____
2. _____   5. _____
3. _____   6. _____

C

Figure out the rules, and write them. Remember to spell the words correctly.

1. a word when the next morphograph begins . . . Drop the final **e** from . . . with a vowel letter

   _____

   _____

2. **cvc** and the next . . . Double the final **c** . . . morphograph begins with **v** . . . in a short word when the word ends

   _____

   _____

Lesson 37

D Circle each short word that ends cvc.
Remember: The letter **x** acts like two consonant letters.

1. stop
2. brother
3. fox
4. mad
5. play
6. buzz
7. rent
8. hot
9. bar
10. box
11. star
12. bare
13. boy
14. water
15. snap

E Add the morphographs together.
Some of the words follow the rule about dropping the final e.

1. write + ing = _____
2. in + value + able = _____
3. late + ly = _____
4. lone + ly = _____
5. force + ful + ly = _____
6. note + able = _____
7. change + ing = _____
8. re + serve + ed = _____

F Each sentence has one misspelled word.
Write each word correctly on the blank.

1. Inform your freinds of my wishes. _____
2. We stayed out all night and studyed the stars. _____
3. I'm tryeing to put plants in all of the rooms. _____

END OF LESSON 37

38 Name _____

A

1. _____
2. _____

B

1. _____ + _____ = _____
2. _____ + _____ = _____
3. _____ + _____ = _____
4. _____ + _____ = _____
5. _____ + _____ = _____
6. _____ + _____ = _____

C

1. _____   6. _____
2. _____   7. _____
3. _____   8. _____
4. _____   9. _____
5. _____   10. _____

D Make 11 real words from the morphographs in the box.

| fine | re | sign | serve | de | con | form |

1. _____   7. _____
2. _____   8. _____
3. _____   9. _____
4. _____   10. _____
5. _____   11. _____
6. _____

E Fill in the blanks to show the morphographs in each word.

1. _____ + _____ + _____ = remaining
2. _____ + _____ + _____ = foolishly
3. _____ + _____ = lonely
4. _____ + _____ = rainy
5. _____ + _____ + _____ + _____ = uninformed
6. _____ + _____ = conform
7. _____ + _____ + _____ = related
8. _____ + _____ = voltage

END OF LESSON 38

Lesson 38

A

show   grow   low   flow   throw   blow   know

B

1. _____   5. _____
2. _____   6. _____
3. _____   7. _____
4. _____   8. _____

C

1. _____ + _____ = _____
2. _____ + _____ = _____
3. _____ + _____ = _____
4. _____ + _____ = _____
5. _____ + _____ = _____
6. _____ + _____ = _____

D

_____
_____
_____
_____
_____
_____
_____
_____
_____
_____

E Figure out the rules, and write them.

1. word ends **cvc** and . . . Double the final **c** in . . . the next morphograph begins with **v** . . . a short word when the

_____

_____

2. word when the next . . . a vowel letter . . . morphograph begins with . . . Drop the final **e** from a

_____

_____

Lesson 39

F Each sentence has one misspelled word. Write each word correctly on the blank.

1. We sprayed twice for weeds along the trial. _____

2. Leave the paches on the inside. _____

3. The children tride to move the boxes. _____

Lesson 40 is a test lesson. There is no worksheet.

Name _____

41

A

1. _____

2. _____

B

1. _____ + _____ = _____

2. _____ + _____ = _____

3. _____ + _____ = _____

4. _____ + _____ = _____

5. _____ + _____ = _____

6. _____ + _____ = _____

C

1. Whose turn is it to make the sines? _____

2. Some people don't think that boxing is a worthy sport. _____

3. She felt sicker from crying and worring so much. _____

Lesson 41   **69**

D These words are in the word search. Circle 7 or more of the words.

denied	patch	date
runner	ease	madder
nail	painter	stored
feel	dented	deny

```
r  d  d  e  n  y  s
n  u  e  a  s  e  t
n  a  n  n  t  e  o
p  a  i  n  t  e  r
f  e  e  l  e  e  e
m  a  d  d  e  r  d
d  a  p  a  t  c  h
```

E Add the morphographs together.

1. un + claim + ed = _____
2. slam + ed = _____
3. con + fine + ing = _____
4. in + still + ed = _____
5. re + act + ing = _____
6. style + ish + ly = _____
7. con + fuse + ing = _____
8. un + luck + y = _____
9. fine + al = _____
10. in + flame + ing = _____
11. leak + age = _____
12. un + read + able = _____

END OF LESSON 41

Name _____

42

A

spray text tract ruin fluid

B

1. __ __ o w
2. __ __ r __ w
3. __ __ __ __
4. __ __ __ __
5. k __ __ __
6. __ l __ __

C

1. _____
2. _____

D

snugness   unbreakable   equally   floating
research   confuse   friendly   storage
deserve   misspelling   stepping   insure

E

1. The trapper found the trale of the foxes.   _____

2. The signs claim that the water is undrinkeable.   _____

3. I plan to confin myself to the inside today.   _____

Lesson 42 **71**

F Cross out the misspelled words in these sentences. Then write the words correctly above the crossed-out words.

Pleaze cloze your books.

There is a valueable packege in the trunk.

G Fill in the blanks to show the morphographs in each word.

1. _____ + _____ + _____ + _____ = undefeated
2. _____ + _____ + _____ = confirmed
3. _____ + _____ = moving
4. _____ + _____ + _____ = removal
5. _____ + _____ = contract
6. _____ + _____ = context
7. _____ + _____ + _____ = instated
8. _____ + _____ = sleepy
9. _____ + _____ = dosage
10. _____ + _____ + _____ = fatally

END OF LESSON 42

Name _____

A

1. _____
2. _____

B Draw a line from each word to its clue.

1. loan • • something done with great skill
2. weather • • by yourself
3. lone • • put words on paper
4. feat • • I will ▮▮▮ you my shirt.
5. whole • • We can't ▮▮▮ your voice.
6. hear • • correct
7. whether • • The ▮▮▮ is good today.
8. write • • change
9. vary • • Do you know ▮▮▮ you will go?
10. right • • I ate a ▮▮▮ cake.

C Each sentence has one misspelled word. Write each word correctly on the blank.

1. She neatly put the defineing stitches on the shirt. _____

2. Figuring out your income taxses can be difficult. _____

3. The unclamed boxes varied in size. _____

Lesson 43   73

D   Figure out the rules, and write them.

1. a word when the next . . . vowel letter . . . Drop the final **e** from . . . morphograph begins with a

   _____

   _____

   _____

2. next morphograph begins with **v** . . . the word ends **cvc** and the . . . **c** in a short word when . . . Double the final

   _____

   _____

   _____

E   Add the morphographs together.

1. glass + es = _____
2. race + s = _____
3. re + tract = _____
4. flat + est = _____
5. note + able = _____
6. in + cure + able = _____
7. con + fine + ing = _____
8. wreck + age = _____
9. globe + al = _____
10. con + test = _____

END OF LESSON 43

Name _____

44

A

1. ___ ___ ___ y ___
2. ___ ___ ___ ___
3. ___ ___ ___ c t
4. ___ u ___ ___
5. ___ ___ ___ i ___

B

1. _____
2. _____
3. _____
4. _____
5. _____
6. _____

C

1. _____ + _____ = _____
2. _____ + _____ = _____
3. _____ + _____ = _____
4. _____ + _____ = _____
5. _____ + _____ = _____
6. _____ + _____ = _____

Lesson 44

D

_____
_____
_____
_____
_____
_____
_____
_____

E Fill in the circle marked **R** if the underlined word is spelled right.
Fill in the circle marked **W** if the underlined word is spelled wrong.

1. We have had very bad <u>weather</u> lately.   (R)   (W)
2. Are you <u>planing</u> a party?   (R)   (W)
3. That was a <u>realy</u> funny story.   (R)   (W)
4. I <u>thought</u> we won the race.   (R)   (W)
5. My sister <u>wrote</u> me a long note.   (R)   (W)
6. Have you <u>studyed</u> for the test?   (R)   (W)

F Each sentence has one misspelled word.
Write each word correctly on the blank.

1. I get depresed easily in bad weather.   _____
2. It's pointless for her to growe long nails.   _____
3. Don't blow on it; it's quite brakeable.   _____

Lesson 45 is a test lesson. There is no worksheet.

76 Lesson 44

Name _____

46

A

Our yellow flowers bloomed early.

_____

B

1. _____ + _____ = _____
2. _____ + _____ = _____
3. _____ + _____ = _____
4. _____ + _____ = _____
5. _____ + _____ = _____
6. _____ + _____ = _____

C Add the morphographs together.

1. con + text = _____
2. ruin + ed = _____
3. con + tract = _____
4. lone + ly = _____
5. un + de + feat + ed = _____
6. fine + al + ly = _____
7. person + al + ly = _____
8. watch + es = _____
9. noise + y = _____
10. trail + er = _____

Lesson 46

D These words are in the word search.
Circle 7 or more of the words.

throw	error	threw
house	large	worry
reach	storage	teach
caught	cure	eight

s	c	a	u	g	h	t
t	t	w	c	c	t	e
e	h	o	u	s	e	a
i	r	r	r	r	r	c
g	o	r	e	a	c	h
h	w	y	o	w	g	a
t	t	l	a	r	g	e

E Each sentence has one misspelled word.
Write each word correctly on the blank.

1. A few reserved seats were remaning for the show. _____

2. I know it's incureable, but I'm unclear as to why. _____

3. The sturdiest rail was foolishley taken down. _____

END OF LESSON 46

Name

A

cause   pause   poison   strange

B

1. _____   4. _____
2. _____   5. _____
3. _____   6. _____

C

Ou_ ye_l_w __ow____ ___oo_ e_ ear__.

_____

D

1. _____   4. _____
2. _____   5. _____
3. _____   6. _____

Lesson 47

E Add the morphographs together.
Some of the words follow the rule about changing y to i.

1. worry + ed = _____

2. pity + ful = _____

3. study + ing = _____

4. play + ful + ly = _____

5. boy + ish + ness = _____

6. try + ed = _____

7. fancy + ful = _____

END OF LESSON 47

Name _____

48

A

1. _____
2. _____

B

1. __ __ u __ __ __
2. __ a __ s __
3. __ __ u g __ __
4. __ o __ __ o __
5. __ a __ __ __
6. __ __ r __ n g __

C

__ u __   y __ __ __ w   __ __ o w __

__ __ __ o __ __   e a __ __.

_____

D

_____
_____
_____
_____
_____
_____
_____
_____

E Fill in the blanks to show the morphographs in each word.

1. _____ + _____ = strangely
2. _____ + _____ = consent
3. _____ + _____ + _____ = presented
4. _____ + _____ + _____ = misplaced
5. _____ + _____ + _____ = winners
6. _____ + _____ + _____ = invaluable
7. _____ + _____ = wonderful
8. _____ + _____ + _____ = reserved

F Each sentence has one misspelled word. Write each word correctly on the blank.

1. Conserve your money, and let it grow, or you'll need a lone. _____

2. Put down that container you're carying. _____

3. The whether forcefully reshaped the land. _____

END OF LESSON 48

Name _____

A

___ ___ ___ y ___ ___ ___ ___ ___ ___ ___ w ___ ___

___ ___ ___ ___ ___ ___ ___ ___ ___ a ___ ___ ___ .

_____

B

1. _____ 4. _____

2. _____ 5. _____

3. _____ 6. _____

C Draw a line from each word to its clue.

1. weather •   • by yourself
2. loan •   • ordinary
3. plain •   • Let's decide ▬▬ or not we will go.
4. right •   • Today's ▬▬ is fine.
5. lone •   • change
6. whether •   • Please ▬▬ me some paint.
7. vary •   • I have a ▬▬ in my shoe.
8. hole •   • You gave the ▬▬ answer.

84 Lesson 49

D Add the morphographs together. Remember to use your spelling rules.

1. early + est = _____
2. con + fine + ment = _____
3. happy + est = _____
4. cloud + y + ness = _____
5. scratch + es = _____
6. pay + ment = _____
7. dark + ness = _____
8. strange + est = _____
9. tough + est = _____
10. grace + ful + ly = _____

E Each sentence has one misspelled word. Write each word correctly on the blank.

1. Todd hopped he would win the baking contest. _____
2. The text is so confusing that it's unreadabal. _____
3. The leeder in all the races is still undefeated. _____

Lesson 50 is a test lesson. There is no worksheet.

51 Name ___

A

1. brain
2. chain
3. drain
4. gain
5. plain
6. rain
7. sprain
8. stain

B

1. ___
2. ___
   ___

C

1. ___
2. ___
3. ___
4. ___
5. ___
6. ___

D Fill in the blanks to show the morphographs in each word.

1. ___ + ___ = stained
2. ___ + ___ = basement
3. ___ + ___ = strangeness
4. ___ + ___ = questionable
5. ___ + ___ = flattest
6. ___ + ___ + ___ = inflaming

E. Circle the misspelled word in each group. Then write it correctly on the line.

1. cloudy
   contract
   pichure
   question
   _____

2. stranger
   driping
   whose
   leader
   _____

3. flowers
   yello
   pause
   regain
   _____

4. lenghten
   package
   movement
   caught
   _____

5. relate
   wonderful
   poisen
   speaker
   _____

6. through
   eight
   people
   helplesness
   _____

7. misspelled
   ruined
   equaly
   mistake
   _____

8. cawze
   valuable
   resources
   confused
   _____

F. Each sentence has one misspelled word. Write each word correctly on the blank.

1. Lateley I have been reading some notable letters. _____

2. She forcefully denied that she was moveing. _____

3. The researcher was confuseed by both parts of the study. _____

END OF LESSON 51

52 Name

A

B

C

spotted	boxes	pause	rainy	straightest
quotable	happiness	yellow	contract	wonderful
throat	cheapest	trail	cause	ruined
together	graceful	speeches	early	resourceful
pleasing	studying	blowing	strange	speaker

D Fill in the blanks to show the morphographs in each word.

1. _____ + _____ + _____ = department
2. _____ + _____ + _____ = confinement
3. _____ + _____ + _____ + _____ = unconfirmed
4. _____ + _____ + _____ = investment
5. _____ + _____ = lucky
6. _____ + _____ = voltage
7. _____ + _____ + _____ = normally
8. _____ + _____ = valuable
9. _____ + _____ + _____ = delightful

E Each sentence has one misspelled word. Write each word correctly on the blank.

1. Instead of sleeping, he studeyed his music lesson. _____

2. By waterring their lawn, they are changing the water force. _____

3. The picture is covered by unbrekable glass. _____

END OF LESSON 52

Lesson 52

53

Name _____

A

1. _____
2. _____

B Figure out the rules, and write them.

1. in a word when the . . . next morphograph begins with . . . word ends consonant-and-**y** and the . . . Change the **y** to **i** . . . anything except **i**

   _____

   _____

   _____

2. with a **v** . . . morphograph begins . . . word when the next . . . Drop the final **e** from a

   _____

   _____

   _____

C **Add the morphographs together. Remember to use your spelling rules.**

1. luck + y + ly = _____
2. early + er = _____
3. strange + er = _____
4. fine + al + ly = _____
5. friend + ly + ness = _____
6. flat + en = _____
7. re + late + ed = _____
8. in + vest + ment + s = _____
9. source + es = _____
10. cloud + y + est = _____

END OF LESSON 53

54 Name _____

A

1. _____ 4. _____
2. _____ 5. _____
3. _____ 6. _____

B

_____
_____
_____
_____
_____
_____
_____
_____
_____

C Each sentence has one misspelled word. Write each word correctly on the blank.

1. The new design made some people feel lonly. _____

2. He denyed removing the contract from our safe. _____

3. He became sleepy as he floted on the raft. _____

Lesson 54

D Make 10 real words from the morphographs in the box.

| en | est | sad | mad | ness | wide | fine |

1. _____
2. _____
3. _____
4. _____
5. _____
6. _____
7. _____
8. _____
9. _____
10. _____

E Fill in the blanks to show the morphographs in each word.

1. _____ + _____ = stranger
2. _____ + _____ = taken
3. _____ + _____ = choicest
4. _____ + _____ = forceful
5. _____ + _____ = signal
6. _____ + _____ + _____ = resigned
7. _____ + _____ + _____ = contracted
8. _____ + _____ + _____ = consignment
9. ____ + ____ + ____ + ____ = unmistakable
10. _____ + _____ + _____ = wonderfully

Lesson 55 is a test lesson. There is no worksheet.

56

Name _____

A

1. _____
2. _____

B Make 14 real words from the morphographs in the box.

| fine | con | de | re | ment | move | ing | ed |

1. _____ 8. _____
2. _____ 9. _____
3. _____ 10. _____
4. _____ 11. _____
5. _____ 12. _____
6. _____ 13. _____
7. _____ 14. _____

C These words are in the word search. Circle 7 or more of the words.

civil	verb	carry
might	deny	robber
gone	dine	match
mad	does	easy

```
c  i  v  i  l  r
m  a  d  e  r  o
a  i  r  i  r  b
t  d  g  r  n  b
c  e  o  h  y  e
h  n  n  e  t  r
m  y  e  a  s  y
```

D Add the morphographs together. Some of the words follow the rule about changing y to i.

1. boy + ish = _____
2. sturdy + ness = _____
3. worry + ed = _____
4. pity + ful = _____
5. sign + al = _____
6. carry + er = _____
7. cry + ing = _____
8. try + al = _____
9. deny + al = _____
10. fly + er = _____

END OF LESSON 56

57 Name _____

A Write contractions for the words below.

1. could not   = _____

2. should not = _____

3. she is   = _____

4. is not   = _____

5. he will   = _____

6. would not   = _____

7. I have   = _____

8. you will   = _____

B

1. _____   4. _____

2. _____   5. _____

3. _____   6. _____

C

Carrying the heavy load is sure to make me breathe hard.

_____

_____

Lesson 57

D Circle the misspelled word in each group. Then write it correctly on the line.

1. other
   wonderfull
   wrong
   could

   _____

2. story
   mispell
   sturdy
   fancy

   _____

3. yellow
   strength
   serve
   strech

   _____

4. author
   poison
   saddness
   civil

   _____

5. dripping
   enuff
   pitch
   normal

   _____

6. peeple
   delightful
   rebuild
   while

   _____

7. valeu
   unthinking
   date
   coldest

   _____

8. useless
   wanted
   worrying
   frends

   _____

END OF LESSON 57

Lesson 57

58 Name _____

A Write contractions for the words below.

1. were not   = _____
2. does not   = _____
3. are not   = _____
4. she will   = _____
5. you have   = _____
6. did not   = _____
7. can not   = _____
8. they are   = _____

B

__ a __ r y __ __ __   __ __ __   __ e a __ y
__ o a __ __ __   __ __   s u r __ __ __
__ __ k __ __   __ __   __ e a __ __ e
__ a __ __ .

_____
_____

C Each sentence has one misspelled word. Write each word correctly on the blank.

1. Five mice will be raceing in the contest.   _____
2. She tryed to find her way out of the darkness.   _____
3. When did you consent to this wonderfull plan?   _____

98   Lesson 58

D Make 10 real words from the morphographs in the box.

| pity | er | ed | fancy | ful | ing | play |

1. _____
2. _____
3. _____
4. _____
5. _____
6. _____
7. _____
8. _____
9. _____
10. _____

E Add the morphographs together.

1. catch + es = _____
2. mis + print + ed = _____
3. un + snap + ed = _____
4. point + less = _____
5. re + serve + ed = _____
6. fit + ness = _____
7. de + light + ful = _____
8. un + de + feat + ed = _____
9. un + vary + ed = _____
10. leak + age = _____
11. speed + y + est = _____
12. ship + ment = _____
13. in + tend + ed = _____
14. con + front = _____

END OF LESSON 58

59   Name _____

A

1. _____
2. _____

B

__ a __ __ y __ __ __   __ __ __   __ e a __ __

__ __ __ __   __ __   __ u r __   __ __

__ __ __ __   __ __   __ __ e a __ __ e

__ __ __ __ .

_____

_____

C   Add the morphographs together.

1. swim + er   = _____
2. fine + est   = _____
3. wide + est   = _____
4. con + sign   = _____
5. mad + ly   = _____
6. rage + ing   = _____
7. trap + er   = _____
8. un + civil + ly = _____

D

Write the word for each meaning. The words will contain these morphographs.

al — related to   **ful** — full of   **est** — the most
pre — before   **ish** — like   **en** — make

1. _____ like a baby
2. _____ the most late
3. _____ related to signs
4. _____ wrap before
5. _____ make light
6. _____ full of care

E

Write contractions for the words below.

1. let us = _____
2. have not = _____
3. was not = _____
4. they will = _____
5. we have = _____
6. what is = _____
7. he is = _____
8. would not = _____

Lesson 60 is a test lesson. There is no worksheet.

61 Name _____

A

___ ___ ___ ___ ___ ___ ___ ___ ___ ___ ___ ___ ___ ___ a ___ ___

___ ___ ___ ___ ___ ___ ___ ___ ___ ___ ___ ___ ___

___ ___ ___ ___ ___ ___ ___ ___ ___ ___ ___ ___ e

___ ___ ___ ___ .

_____

_____

B Complete each sentence correctly with one of these words:

> write   right

1. My grandmother likes it when I _____ long letters.
2. Janis is the _____ person for the job.
3. My answers on the test were all _____ .
4. When Martin was four years old, he could _____ his name.

C Write contractions for the words below.

1. has not = _____
2. you are = _____
3. we will = _____
4. are not = _____
5. I will = _____
6. they are = _____
7. were not = _____
8. it is = _____

D Circle the misspelled word in each group. Then write it correctly on the line.

1. worry
   brother
   might
   civel

2. catch
   friend
   wandor
   change

3. hurring
   fitness
   preview
   ruined

4. claim
   queit
   choice
   equal

_____   _____   _____   _____

E Fill in the blanks to show the morphographs in each word.

1. _____ + _____ + _____ + _____ = unrefined
2. _____ + _____ + _____ = packaging
3. _____ + _____ + _____ = rightfully
4. _____ + _____ = inhuman
5. _____ + _____ + _____ = strengthening
6. _____ + _____ + _____ = loneliness
7. _____ + _____ + _____ = helplessness
8. _____ + _____ + _____ = unequally
9. _____ + _____ + _____ = resigned
10. _____ + _____ + _____ + _____ = unrelated

END OF LESSON 61

A

1. _____

2. _____

B

1. _____ 5. _____
2. _____ 6. _____
3. _____ 7. _____
4. _____ 8. _____

C

Complete each sentence correctly with one of these words:

weather   clothes   very   sale   would

1. Are those toys for _____ ?

2. That rack is _____ heavy.

3. The _____ has been cold and rainy all week.

4. Do you know which _____ he wore?

5. I _____ stay longer if I had more time.

6. Our spelling test was _____ easy.

D Write contractions for the words below.

1. should not = _____
2. she is   = _____
3. I have   = _____
4. what is = _____
5. they will = _____
6. we are   = _____

E Figure out the rules, and write them.

1. in a short word when the . . . next morphograph begins with **v** . . . Double the final **c** . . . word ends **cvc** and the

   _____

   _____

   _____

2. consonant-and-**y** and the . . . a word when the word ends . . . next morphograph begins with anything except **i** . . . Change the **y** to **i** in

   _____

   _____

   _____

F Each sentence has one misspelled word. Write each word correctly on the blank.

1. The fish seemed confused and was spining around in the water.   _____

2. Such a large dosege is unproven and may be harmful.   _____

3. They were hopeful as they planed a delightful party.   _____

END OF LESSON 62

63 Name _____

A

1. _____ + _____ = _____
2. _____ + _____ + _____ = _____
3. _____ + _____ = _____
4. _____ + _____ = _____
5. _____ + _____ = _____
6. _____ + _____ = _____
7. _____ + _____ = _____
8. _____ + _____ = _____

B

1. _____
   _____
2. _____
   _____

C Write contractions for the words below.

1. can not = _____
2. does not = _____
3. they will = _____
4. you have = _____
5. are not = _____
6. what is = _____
7. it is = _____
8. let us = _____

D Make 11 real words from the morphographs in the box.

| friend | ly | happy | ness | lone | sturdy | est |

1. _____
2. _____
3. _____
4. _____
5. _____
6. _____
7. _____
8. _____
9. _____
10. _____
11. _____

E Fill in the blanks to show the morphographs in each word.

1. _____ + _____ = sadder
2. _____ + _____ = strengthen
3. _____ + _____ + _____ = informal
4. _____ + _____ = useful
5. _____ + _____ = express
6. _____ + _____ + _____ = reserving
7. _____ + _____ + _____ = defacing
8. _____ + _____ = planning

There are no worksheets for Lesson 64 and Lesson 65.

Lesson 63   **107**

66 Name

A

1. _____ + _____ = _____
2. _____ + _____ = _____
3. _____ + _____ = _____
4. _____ + _____ = _____
5. _____ + _____ = _____
6. _____ + _____ = _____
7. _____ + _____ = _____
8. _____ + _____ = _____

B

C. Add the morphographs together.

1. re + move + al = _____
2. in + come = _____
3. rise + ing = _____
4. safe + ly = _____
5. hot + est = _____
6. mad + ness = _____
7. un + de + serve + ing = _____
8. use + age = _____
9. verb + al + ly = _____
10. re + cent + ly = _____
11. swim + er = _____
12. real + ly = _____

D. Cross out the misspelled words in these sentences. Then write the words correctly above the crossed-out words.

Sevral stranje birds landed togather.

We are'nt leaving the main road.

That was the greatest feet of strenght I've seen.

END OF LESSON 66

67 Name _____

A

1. _____   4. _____
2. _____   5. _____
3. _____   6. _____

B

1. __ __ o __ __   4. __ __ __ __ __
2. __ __ __ u __   5. __ __ __ w __
3. __ __ u __ __   6. __ __ __ __ __

C

These words are in the word search.
Circle 7 or more of the words.

brotherly   length
spotted   whether
neat   report
loud   race
stay   traps
vary   cared

```
b  r  c  l  s  n  t  l  w
r  r  n  a  o  u  u  e  h
s  e  o  n  r  u  o  n  e
s  p  o  t  t  e  d  g  t
s  o  a  y  h  n  d  t  h
s  r  a  c  e  e  e  h  e
l  t  r  a  p  s  r  a  r
v  t  a  t  o  r  t  l  t
v  a  r  y  y  r  h  h  y
```

110 Lesson 67

D Complete each sentence correctly with these words:

weather   vary   write   they're   right   whole

1. Tony's new shoes are exactly the _____ size.

2. Instead of eating the same thing all the time, you should _____ your diet.

3. My uncle was so hungry last Sunday that he ate a _____ chicken.

4. The farmers aren't worried. _____ expecting good _____.

5. Joggers don't usually run at the same speed all the time. They usually _____ their pace.

6. The blanks on your worksheet are where you _____ spelling words.

7. Last Friday we worked the _____ day.

E Each sentence has one misspelled word. Write each word correctly on the blank.

1. Our investments were confirmed to be very valueble. _____

2. Who wrote the best ansuers to the questions? _____

3. What caused you to buy that strange painte? _____

END OF LESSON 67

Name _____

A

    quick   quiz   quest

B

1. _____
2. _____

C

1. _____ 5. _____
2. _____ 6. _____
3. _____ 7. _____
4. _____ 8. _____

D

Write **s** or **es** in the second column. Then add the morphographs together.

            s or **es**

1. glass   + _____ = _____
2. reach   + _____ = _____
3. sound   + _____ = _____
4. brush   + _____ = _____
5. scratch + _____ = _____
6. flower + _____ = _____

E Fill in the blanks to show the morphographs in each word.

1. _____ + _____ + _____ = explained
2. _____ + _____ = resource
3. _____ + _____ = movement
4. _____ + _____ + _____ + _____ = unrelated
5. _____ + _____ + _____ + _____ = unconfirmed
6. _____ + _____ + _____ = informer
7. _____ + _____ + _____ = childishly
8. _____ + _____ + _____ = noisiness

F Each sentence has one misspelled word. Write each word correctly on the blank.

1. The flowers and birds made a lovely pickture together. _____

2. The movment of the ship caused me to feel dizzy. _____

3. After twenty years she finaly said that she would resign. _____

END OF LESSON 68

Lesson 68 **113**

69

Name _____

A

1. __ __ e __
2. __ u __ __
3. __ __ e __ __
4. __ __ __ t __
5. __ __ __ o __ __
6. __ __ __ c __

B

_____
_____
_____
_____
_____
_____
_____
_____
_____

C

Cross out the misspelled words in these sentences. Then write the words correctly above the crossed-out words.

We worryed uselesly about the whether.

My frend chandges his cloze offen.

D

1. their
2. here
3. vary
4. close
5. sale
6. loan
7. they're
8. write
9. feet
10. weather

- She forgot to ▮ the window.
- contraction of **they are**
- Can you ▮ me some money?
- The students exchanged ▮ papers.
- change
- The ▮ has been good lately.
- My ▮ were sore after the hike.
- We moved ▮ a year ago.
- Our car is for ▮ .
- I can ▮ two words in Spanish.

Lesson 70 is a test lesson. There is no worksheet.

71 Name _____

A

One athlete finished the contest before everyone else.

_____

_____

B

1. _____   7. _____

2. _____   8. _____

3. _____   9. _____

4. _____   10. _____

5. _____   11. _____

6. _____   12. _____

C Write contractions for the words below.

1. it is   = _____   5. can not = _____

2. are not   = _____   6. let us   = _____

3. that is   = _____   7. you will = _____

4. would not = _____   8. we have = _____

D. Add the morphographs together.

1. re + quest = _____
2. win + er = _____
3. pity + ful = _____
4. strength + en + ing = _____
5. un + ex + plain + ed = _____
6. de + feat + ed = _____
7. re + place + ment = _____
8. con + front + ed = _____
9. nudge + ing = _____
10. star + ing = _____
11. ripe + ness = _____
12. straight + est = _____

E. Each sentence has one misspelled word. Write each word correctly on the blank.

1. It is unlikely that they will remain peacful. _____
2. They presented questions about the leakags from the pipes. _____
3. Which department store serves the best refereshments? _____

END OF LESSON 71

72

A

O__e e____ ___lete
___i s h_d ___
___n___st __f__re
__ve __yo__ __e__se.

B

C. Make 9 real words from the morphographs in the box.

| ed | form | re | in | er | con |

1. _____
2. _____
3. _____
4. _____
5. _____
6. _____
7. _____
8. _____
9. _____

D. Figure out the rules, and write them.

1. in a short word when the . . . Double the final c . . . morphograph begins with v . . . word ends cvc and the next

   _____

   _____

2. with anything except i . . . and the next morphograph begins . . . when the word ends consonant-and-y . . . to i in a word . . . Change the y

   _____

   _____

END OF LESSON 72

A

danger   beauty   sudden   cover

B

1. _____
2. _____

C

1. _____   5. _____
2. _____   6. _____
3. _____   7. _____
4. _____   8. _____

D Write the contractions for the words below.

1. could not   = _____
2. it is   = _____
3. are not   = _____
4. we will   = _____
5. you will   = _____
6. let us   = _____
7. you have   = _____
8. does not   = _____

E Draw a line from each word to its clue.

1. peace • • by yourself
2. their • • belonging to them
3. whole • • We think ▐▐▐ coming home soon.
4. lone • • no fighting
5. they're • • My answer wasn't ▐▐▐ .
6. right • • We ate a ▐▐▐ loaf of bread.

F Each sentence has one misspelled word. Write each word correctly on the blank.

1. We thought that they caught seaveral fish. _____

2. She is a resourcful shopper and makes wise investments. _____

3. The early reports about the risks of ruining the land were misstaken. _____

END OF LESSON 73

74

Name _____

A

1. __ e a __ __ __
2. __ u __ __ __
3. __ __ __ e __

4. __ __ __ g __ __
5. __ __ __ d __ __
6. q __ __ __ __

B

1. _____
2. _____
3. _____
4. _____
5. _____

6. _____
7. _____
8. _____
9. _____
10. _____

C

Cross out the misspelled words in these sentences. Then write the words correctly above the crossed-out words.

There arn't enugh resorces for that plan.

The happyest childern wern't realy rich.

Lesson 74

D. Write s or es in the second column. Then add the morphographs together.

s or es

1. world + _____ = _____
2. stretch + _____ = _____
3. research + _____ = _____
4. wash + _____ = _____
5. light + _____ = _____
6. tax + _____ = _____
7. class + _____ = _____
8. refresh + _____ = _____

E. Complete each sentence correctly with one of these words:

write   right

1. Do you have the _____ time?
2. I started to _____ my report early.
3. Be sure to _____ your name on all your work.
4. We finally found the _____ house.
5. My dad has a scar on his _____ hand.

Lesson 75 is a test lesson. There is no worksheet.

76

A

O___ ___ete ___is___ ___ ___s_ ___ore ___ery_e___e.

B

1. _____ 5. _____
2. _____ 6. _____
3. _____ 7. _____
4. _____ 8. _____

C

D. Fill in the blanks to show the morphographs in each word.

1. _____ + _____ + _____ = confinement
2. _____ + _____ + _____ = wonderfully
3. _____ + _____ + _____ = requesting
4. _____ + _____ + _____ = unquotable
5. _____ + _____ + _____ = explained
6. _____ + _____ = stranger
7. _____ + _____ = poisoning
8. _____ + _____ = context
9. _____ + _____ + _____ = cloudiness

E. Each sentence has one misspelled word. Write each word correctly on the blank.

1. We were impressed with the friendlyness of the stranger. _____

2. Some people like to go shoping on the cloudiest days. _____

3. You can clearly hear her greatness in her speechs. _____

END OF LESSON 76

77

A

chief　　　niece　　　grief　　　brief　　　thief

B

_ _ _ _ _ _ e t e

_ _ _ _ _ _ e_ _ _ _

_ _ _ _ _ _ _ _ _ o r e

_ _ e_ y _ _ _ _ _ _.

C

126　Lesson 77

D Add the morphographs together.
Remember to use your spelling rules.

1. beauty + ful = _____
2. sudden + ly = _____
3. peace + ful + ly = _____
4. ex + change + ing = _____
5. in + vest + ment = _____
6. con + tact + ed = _____
7. re + strict + ed = _____
8. noise + y = _____
9. fine + al + ly = _____
10. volt + age = _____
11. grip + ing = _____

END OF LESSON 77

78

A

___ ___ e __ e

_____ ___

_____ _____ e

__ e _____ ____.

B

1. __ r __ e __
2. __ i __ c __
3. __ __ i __ __
4. __ __ __ __ __
5. __ h __ __ __

C

D
Circle the misspelled word in each group. Then write it correctly on the line.

1. worryed
   crying
   denied
   playful

   _____

2. chalky
   children
   cheepest
   changing

   _____

3. spotless
   maddness
   winner
   shopping

   _____

4. straight
   stretch
   strenght
   switch

   _____

5. really
   filling
   nicely
   civily

   _____

6. thought
   enough
   thrugh
   question

   _____

E
Each sentence has one misspelled word. Write each word correctly on the blank.

1. His plan might riune the delightful trail.   _____

2. They were not joyful as they studyed the report.   _____

3. She greatly improved the wraping paper.   _____

END OF LESSON 78

A

govern   reason   type   house   first

B

1. _____   5. _____
2. _____   6. _____
3. _____   7. _____
4. _____   8. _____

C

1. _____
2. _____

D

Circle the short cvc words.

Remember: Short words have four letters or fewer.
The letter **y** is a vowel letter at the end of a morphograph.
The letter **x** acts like two consonant letters.

1. sudden   4. trip   7. grab   10. reason
2. boy   5. poison   8. spot   11. cover
3. chin   6. box   9. hid   12. flat

E Fill in the blanks to show the morphographs in each word.

1. _____ + _____ + _____ = defining
2. _____ + _____ = final
3. _____ + _____ + _____ = confinement
4. _____ + _____ + _____ = designer
5. _____ + _____ + _____ = resigned
6. _____ + _____ = signal
7. _____ + _____ + _____ + _____ = unrecoverable
8. _____ + _____ = heaviest

Lesson 80 is a test lesson. There is no worksheet.

A

1. __ y __ __
2. __ i __ __ __
3. __ o __ e r __
4. __ e a __ o __
5. __ __ u s __

B

1. _____
   _____

2. _____
   _____

C

1. _____   4. _____
2. _____   5. _____
3. _____   6. _____

D Complete each sentence correctly with one of these words.

peace   there   they're   piece   their

1. The boys are staying home because _____ sick.

2. Please put those books over _____ , on the shelf.

3. Someone gave us each a _____ of pie.

4. I enjoy the _____ and quiet of the lake.

5. Mr. and Mrs. Sato lost _____ dog.

6. We all wrote a thank-you note on one _____ of paper.

7. Matt and Kim went fishing yesterday. _____ going again today.

8. I went to your house, but you weren't _____ .

END OF LESSON 81

82

Name _____

A

Our second surprise was especially exciting.

_____

_____

B

s or **es**

1. worry + _____ = _____
2. story + _____ = _____
3. try + _____ = _____
4. joy + _____ = _____
5. copy + _____ = _____
6. boy + _____ = _____
7. play + _____ = _____
8. study + _____ = _____
9. stay + _____ = _____
10. carry + _____ = _____

C Circle the misspelled word in each group. Then write it correctly on the line.

1. proud
   strength
   mispelled
   wrong
   _____

2. wander
   equil
   answer
   friendly
   _____

3. auther
   hurry
   sturdy
   reason
   _____

4. pleaze
   straight
   whose
   niece
   _____

5. danger
   should
   happiness
   realy
   _____

6. rezerve
   house
   swimmer
   chief
   _____

END OF LESSON 82

A

__ _ c o _ d
_ u r _ _ i s e ___
e __ e c i a l __
_ x c _ t _ n g .

B

s or **es**

1. stay + _____ = _____
2. copy + _____ = _____
3. toy + _____ = _____
4. spray + _____ = _____
5. worry + _____ = _____
6. fly + _____ = _____
7. boy + _____ = _____
8. carry + _____ = _____

C. Fill in the blanks to show the morphographs in each word.

1. _____ + _____ + _____ = prolonged
2. _____ + _____ = express
3. _____ + _____ + _____ = profoundly
4. _____ + _____ + _____ = refinement
5. _____ + _____ + _____ = exported
6. _____ + _____ = conserve
7. _____ + _____ + _____ + _____ = unrelated
8. _____ + _____ = briefly

D. Add the morphographs together.

1. govern + ment = _____
2. rise + ing = _____
3. trap + ed = _____
4. straight + en = _____
5. reason + able = _____
6. un + type + ed = _____
7. carry + ed = _____
8. strength + en = _____
9. force + ful = _____
10. beauty + ful + ly = _____

E Each sentence has one misspelled word. Write each word correctly on the blank.

1. How many people are in the buisness of exporting food? _____

2. She presented us with a wunderful display of flowers. _____

3. How did the boxes of brushs get in the bushes? _____

END OF LESSON 83

Name _____ 84

A

___ ___ ___   ___ ___ o ___ ___

___ ___ r ___ ___ ___ s ___   ___ ___ ___

___ ___ ___ ___ c i a ___ ___ ___

___ x c ___ ___ ___ ___ .

_____

_____

B   s or es

1. boy + _____ = _____

2. story + _____ = _____

3. try + _____ = _____

4. worry + _____ = _____

5. stay + _____ = _____

6. fly + _____ = _____

7. study + _____ = _____

8. carry + _____ = _____

C

shouldn't	caught	replacement	chiefly	watching
together	believe	answer	house	conserve
different	exchange	govern	greatest	school
children	safely	person	signal	hurried

D Complete each sentence correctly with these words:

would	write	they're	whole	their
very	vary	right	hole	

1. Parachute jumping is a _____ exciting sport.

2. Whenever you misspell a word, you should _____ that word correctly at least one time.

3. A woodpecker made a small _____ in the side of our barn.

4. The boys are late because _____ helping Mrs. Olmsted.

5. No one thought Sandy _____ finish her book, but she read the _____ story anyway.

6. The Marche Company hasn't hired a shipping clerk because they haven't found the _____ person for the job.

7. I do different exercises every day. My friends also _____ _____ exercises.

Lesson 85 is a test lesson. There is no worksheet.

Name _____

A
s or **es**

1. study + _____ = _____
2. story + _____ = _____
3. play + _____ = _____
4. glory + _____ = _____
5. cry + _____ = _____
6. joy + _____ = _____
7. city + _____ = _____
8. fly + _____ = _____

B

1. _____
  _____
2. _____

C

1. _____   4. _____
2. _____   5. _____
3. _____   6. _____

Lesson 86

D

listen	proclaim	reason	style
largest	sleepy	search	picture
school	pitiful	question	straight

E Make 11 real words from the morphographs in the box.

> hot   ly   sturdy   er   mad   nasty   est

1. _____
2. _____
3. _____
4. _____
5. _____
6. _____
7. _____
8. _____
9. _____
10. _____
11. _____

F Each sentence has one misspelled word. Write each word correctly on the blank.

1. Our restlessness grew because of the countles delays. _____

2. The noise they made proved how thougtless they are. _____

3. The speeker misquoted the remarks we made. _____

There is no worksheet for Lesson 87.

Lesson 86

Name _____

A

show   water   know   law   whether   blow

B s or es

1. copy + _____ = _____

2. spray + _____ = _____

3. fly + _____ = _____

4. boy + _____ = _____

5. city + _____ = _____

6. worry + _____ = _____

7. study + _____ = _____

8. story + _____ = _____

C Write contractions for the words below.

1. were not = _____   5. let us = _____

2. have not = _____   6. are not = _____

3. you will = _____   7. would not = _____

4. they had = _____   8. does not = _____

Lesson 88

D Fill in the blanks to show the morphographs in each word.

1. _____ + _____ = relate

2. _____ + _____ + _____ = relative

3. _____ + _____ + _____ = expressive

4. _____ + _____ = moving

5. _____ + _____ + _____ = removal

6. _____ + _____ = proverb

7. _____ + _____ = react

8. _____ + _____ + _____ = reaction

END OF LESSON 88

Name _____

89

A

1. _____

_____

2. _____

B

1. _____ 4. _____

2. _____ 5. _____

3. _____ 6. _____

C

Lesson 89

D Write <u>s</u> or <u>es</u> in the second column. Then add the morphographs together.

s or es

1. tax + _____ = _____
2. study + _____ = _____
3. play + _____ = _____
4. brush + _____ = _____
5. reason + _____ = _____
6. copy + _____ = _____
7. thought + _____ = _____
8. worry + _____ = _____
9. spray + _____ = _____
10. baby + _____ = _____

E Each sentence has one misspelled word. Write each word correctly on the blank.

1. They exchanged the other exportes for unrefined oil.   _____
2. It would be foolish to copy an unprooven plan.   _____
3. The bigest values are found in department stores.   _____

Lesson 90 is a test lesson. There is no worksheet.

146   Lesson 89

Name _____

A

1. _____   4. _____
2. _____   5. _____
3. _____   6. _____

B Circle each short word that ends <u>cvc</u>.

1. reason   4. win   7. form   10. cover
2. stop   5. snap   8. fit   11. spin
3. grow   6. boy   9. stay   12. big

C Add the morphographs together.

1. please + ing   = _____
2. worry + es   = _____
3. neat + ness   = _____
4. study + ed   = _____
5. sad + ness   = _____
6. re + late + ive   = _____
7. story + es   = _____
8. fit + ing   = _____
9. pity + ful   = _____
10. wrap + er   = _____

Lesson 91

D **Figure out the rules, and write them.**

1. **c** in a short word when . . . morphograph begins with **v** . . . the word ends . . . Double the final . . . **cvc** and the next

   _____

   _____

   _____

2. a word when the word ends . . . next morphograph begins with anything except **i** . . . consonant-and-**y** and the . . . Change the **y** to **i** in

   _____

   _____

   _____

END OF LESSON 91

Name _____

92

A

1. _____
2. _____
3. _____
4. _____
5. _____
6. _____
7. _____

B

1. _____
2. _____
3. _____
4. _____
5. _____
6. _____

C Make 11 real words from the morphographs in the box.

| less | thought | ness | hope | ly | ful |

1. _____
2. _____
3. _____
4. _____
5. _____
6. _____
7. _____
8. _____
9. _____
10. _____
11. _____

Lesson 92   149

D Complete each sentence correctly with these words:

| write | feat | their | hole |
| whole | vary | right | threw |

1. The detective thinks that she is not telling the _____ truth.

2. Jan swam across the raging river, which was a brave _____ .

3. I used to print my name, but now I _____ it.

4. The restaurants on Miller Street are popular because they _____ their menus daily.

5. A strong man at the circus performed a different _____ of strength during every show.

6. The students checked _____ answers. Every student got every answer _____ .

7. We _____ beanbags through a _____ in the wall.

E Each sentence has one misspelled word. Write each word correctly on the blank.

1. The queen stopped worying about her quest for golden things.   _____

2. The children raced playfully into the swiming pool.   _____

3. Suddenly we found out that we were near danjer.   _____

END OF LESSON 92

Name _____

93

A

1. _____ 4. _____

2. _____ 5. _____

3. _____ 6. _____

B

1. _____

2. _____

3. _____

4. _____

_____

C

power   doubt   price   guide   name   breath

Lesson 93 151

D Write contractions for the words below.

1. what is = _____
2. would not = _____
3. can not = _____
4. they have = _____
5. he will = _____
6. are not = _____
7. it is = _____
8. they are = _____

E Add the morphographs together.

1. bench + es = _____
2. try + es = _____
3. nice + ly = _____
4. early + er = _____
5. copy + es = _____
6. happy + ness = _____
7. worry + ed = _____
8. stay + s = _____

END OF LESSON 93

Name

A

1. _____ 4. _____
2. _____ 5. _____
3. _____ 6. _____

B

1. _____
2. _____
   _____

C

fashion   fair   solve   tribe   rich   globe

D

These words are in the word search. Circle 7 or more of the words.

station   headed
business   form
night   fires
depart   equal
stress   meet
ruin   farms

```
m  h  s  s  f  f  f  f
m  e  e  t  t  o  i  a
d  e  p  a  r  t  r  r
r  q  t  t  d  e  e  m
b  u  s  i  n  e  s  s
h  a  i  o  s  s  d  s
s  l  i  n  i  g  h  t
```

Lesson 94 153

E Fill in the blanks to show the morphographs in each word.

1. _____ + _____ = request
2. _____ + _____ = powerful
3. _____ + _____ = conquest
4. _____ + _____ = varied
5. _____ + _____ = various
6. _____ + _____ = doubtless
7. _____ + _____ = lately
8. _____ + _____ + _____ = relation

F Each sentence has one misspelled word. Write each word correctly on the blank.

1. He was breething hard before the contest began. _____

2. The teacher asked the students to finnish their papers. _____

3. I wrote a story about a loveable athlete. _____

Lesson 95 is a test lesson. There is no worksheet.

Name _____

A

Nineteen athletes exercised throughout the morning.

_____

_____

B

1. _____   4. _____
2. _____   5. _____
3. _____   6. _____

C

D Add the morphographs together.

1. danger + ous = _____
2. worth + y + ness = _____
3. quest + ion + able = _____
4. doubt + ful + ly = _____
5. probe + ing = _____
6. like + ly + ness = _____
7. re + solve = _____
8. note + ion = _____
9. carry + age = _____
10. fashion + able = _____
11. try + al = _____
12. con + tract + ion = _____

END OF LESSON 96

Name _____   **97**

A

1. _____   4. _____

2. _____   5. _____

3. _____   6. _____

B

1. _____ + _____ = _____

2. _____ + _____ = _____

3. _____ + _____ = _____

4. _____ + _____ = _____

5. _____ + _____ = _____

6. _____ + _____ = _____

C

__ __ e t e __ __   __ t __ l e t __ __

__ __ e __ c __ s __ __

__ __ __ o u g __ o __ __ __ __ __

__ o r __ __ __ __ __ .

_____

_____

Lesson 97

D **Draw a line from each word to its clue.**

1. would • • in that place

2. there • • My friends save ▮ money.

3. here • • We had a ▮ good lunch.

4. hear • • contraction of **they are**

5. very • • How ▮ you like a surprise?

6. plain • • We expect better ▮ tomorrow.

7. they're • • Please speak louder. I can't ▮ you.

8. their • • in this place

9. weather • • part of something

10. piece • • ordinary

END OF LESSON 97

Name _____

98

A

1. _____ 4. _____

2. _____ 5. _____

3. _____ 6. _____

B

1. _____ + _____ = _____

2. _____ + _____ = _____

3. _____ + _____ = _____

4. _____ + _____ = _____

5. _____ + _____ = _____

6. _____ + _____ = _____

C

Lesson 98 **159**

D

__ __ __ e __ __ __   __ __ __ l e __ __ __

__ __ e __ c __ __ __

__ __ __ o u __ __ __ __   __ __ __

__ o __ __ __ __ .

E **Figure out the rules, and write them.**

1. with anything except **i** . . . the next morphograph begins . . . **i** in a word when the . . . Change the **y** to . . . word ends consonant-and-**y** and

2. with **v** . . . morphograph begins . . . word when the next . . . final **e** from a . . . Drop the

F **Each sentence has one misspelled word. Write each word correctly on the blank.**

1. We could not believe her graceful baeuty. _____

2. How piecefully the goats walked along the stony trail! _____

3. Be carefull not to misjudge what the class wrote. _____

END OF LESSON 98

99 Name

A

scribe　　store　　fright　　tough　　short　　loose

B

1. _____

2. _____

C

1. __ __ u b __
2. __ __ s h __ __ __
3. __ u __ __ __
4. __ o l __ __
5. __ o __ e __
6. __ __ __ __ i __ h __

162　Lesson 99

D Add the morphographs together.

1. un + fair + ly = _____
2. drip + ing = _____
3. hard + en + ed = _____
4. room + y + ness = _____
5. joy + ful + ly = _____
6. un + de + feat + ed = _____
7. tense + ion = _____
8. in + tense + ive = _____
9. glory + ous = _____
10. pro + vise + ion = _____

Lesson 100 is a test lesson. There is no worksheet.

101 Name _____

A

script   tone   crease   shrink   tense   treat

B

People weren't interested in the photograph.

_____

_____

C Complete each sentence correctly with these words:

their	where	through	threw
whether	eight	loan	tale

1. I had _____ good reasons for staying home.

2. They wanted to _____ me some money, but _____ pockets were empty.

3. We have to decide _____ or not we will go.

4. Mr. Samuels told us a _____ about a man who forgot _____ he lived one day.

5. We saw him _____ the window.

6. The girls _____ a few pebbles into the river.

7. Ivan and Roberta started _____ own business.

D **Add the morphographs together.**

1. try + al = _____
2. con + tract + ion = _____
3. re + late + ive + ly = _____
4. city + es = _____
5. un + like + ly + ness = _____
6. ex + press + ion = _____
7. beauty + ful + ly = _____
8. noise + y + ness = _____
9. re + cent + ly = _____
10. in + cure + able = _____
11. un + ex + plain + ed = _____
12. re + late + ion = _____

END OF LESSON 101

102

Name _____

A

1. _____
2. _____
3. _____
4. _____

B

1. _____   4. _____
2. _____   5. _____
3. _____   6. _____

C

D

__ e o __ l __   __ __ r e __ ' __
__ __ t e r   __ t __ __   __ __   __ __ __
p __ __ __ o __ __ p h .

_____

_____

E **Cross out the misspelled words in these sentences. Then write the words correctly above the crossed-out words.**

I could'nt here the teecher.

The whether has been beautyful this weck.

How many storys will the author right?

F **Each sentence has one misspelled word. Write each word correctly on the blank.**

1. We will replace the sourses of income we lost. _____

2. They ignored our request for replasement parts. _____

3. She spent hours wrapping those wonderful pakages. _____

END OF LESSON 102

103   Name _____

A

1. _____ + _____ = _____
2. _____ + _____ = _____
3. _____ + _____ = _____
4. _____ + _____ = _____
5. _____ + _____ = _____
6. _____ + _____ = _____

B

1. _____
2. _____

C

D

__ __ o __ __ __ __   __ __ __ e __ __ '__

__ __ __ e __ r __ __ __ __ __ __   __ __   __ __ __

__ __ __ __ __ __ __ __ p __ .

E Write <u>s</u> or <u>es</u> in the second column.
Then add the morphographs together.

                   s or es

1. scratch + _____ = _____
2. copy + _____ = _____
3. wash + _____ = _____
4. boy + _____ = _____
5. fly + _____ = _____
6. hurry + _____ = _____
7. dress + _____ = _____
8. plan + _____ = _____

END OF LESSON 103

A

1. _____

2. _____

B

settle   agree   spirit   thirst   strict

C

1. _____   3. _____

2. _____   4. _____

D Each sentence has one misspelled word. Write each word correctly on the blank.

1. Tom was finally defeeted in the last contest.   _____

2. The quiz had some questions I couln't answer.   _____

3. We questioned the soundness of their statments.   _____

E. Add the morphographs together.

1. un + in + form + ed = _____
2. rate + ion = _____
3. re + strict + ed = _____
4. peace + ful + ly = _____
5. fury + ous = _____
6. re + late + ive + ly = _____
7. in + act + ive = _____
8. study + ous = _____
9. pro + port + ion = _____
10. create + ive = _____

F. Fill in the blanks to show the morphographs in each word.

1. _____ + _____ = snapping
2. _____ + _____ = rightful
3. _____ + _____ + _____ = depression
4. _____ + _____ + _____ = actively
5. _____ + _____ = various
6. _____ + _____ + _____ = proclaimed

Lesson 105 is a test lesson. There is no worksheet.

A

Anybody would rather be healthy instead of rich.

_____

_____

B

1. _____   3. _____

2. _____   4. _____

C

1. _____   3. _____

2. _____   4. _____

D Write the correct spelling for each word.
Then write one of these letters after each number:

Write **O** if the word is spelled by just putting the morphographs together.
Write **A** if the final-**e** rule explains why the spelling is changed.
Write **B** if the doubling rule explains why the spelling is changed.
Write **C** if the **y**-to-**i** rule explains why the spelling is changed.

1. _____ hurry + ed = _____

2. _____ carry + ing = _____

3. _____ trap + er = _____

4. _____ happy + ness = _____

5. _____ ease + y = _____

6. _____ proud + ly = _____

7. _____ late + ly = _____

8. _____ tense + ion = _____

9. _____ clap + ing = _____

END OF LESSON 106

Lesson 106 **173**

107 Name _____

A

_ _ _ _ _ o _ _   _ o u l _
_ a _ _ e r   _ _   _ e a l _ _ _
_ _ _ _ e a _   _ _   _ _ c _ .

_____

_____

B Circle the misspelled word in each group. Then write it correctly on the line.

1. fashion
   poison
   strate
   rather
   _____

2. glory
   pleaze
   place
   settle
   _____

3. brother
   wrong
   carry
   hopeing
   _____

4. prove
   cawse
   hurried
   agree
   _____

5. crease
   change
   request
   ninteen
   _____

6. choice
   sorce
   strength
   studying
   _____

7. sturdyness
   recover
   serve
   priceless
   _____

8. swimmer
   serving
   pitiful
   lowwer
   _____

174   Lesson 107

C Write the correct spelling for each word.
Then write one of these letters after each number:

Write **O** if the word is spelled by just putting the morphographs together.

Write **A** if the final-**e** rule explains why the spelling is changed.

Write **B** if the doubling rule explains why the spelling is changed.

Write **C** if the **y**-to-**i** rule explains why the spelling is changed.

1. _____ low + er = _____

2. _____ snap + ed = _____

3. _____ store + age = _____

4. _____ edge + y = _____

5. _____ slip + ing = _____

6. _____ move + ment = _____

7. _____ fit + ness = _____

8. _____ flaw + ed = _____

9. _____ note + ion = _____

10. _____ play + ing = _____

11. _____ run + y = _____

12. _____ like + able = _____

Lesson 107

D Fill in the blanks to show the morphographs in each word.

1. _____ + _____ + _____ = repressive
2. _____ + _____ + _____ = depression
3. _____ + _____ + _____ = expressed
4. _____ + _____ = feature
5. _____ + _____ + _____ = defeated
6. _____ + _____ = passion
7. _____ + _____ + _____ = profoundly
8. _____ + _____ + _____ = invaluable

END OF LESSON 107

Name _____ 108

A
Write <u>s</u> or <u>es</u> in the second column.
Then add the morphographs together.

                    s or es

1. press   + _____ = _____

2. shop   + _____ = _____

3. buzz   + _____ = _____

4. box   + _____ = _____

5. stretch + _____ = _____

6. rich   + _____ = _____

7. wash   + _____ = _____

8. script + _____ = _____

B

_ _ _ _ o _ _   _ _ _ _

_ _ _ _ e _   _ _   _ _ a _ _

_ _ _ _ _ a _   _ _   _ _ _ _ .

_____

_____

Lesson 108   **177**

C

1. _____   4. _____
2. _____   5. _____
3. _____

D Write the correct word for each sentence.

1. The **weather/whether** has been great.   _____

2. They found **their/there** things.   _____

3. We **through/threw** rocks in the lake.   _____

4. Pat ate **to/too** much.   _____

5. Please bring those books **hear/here**.   _____

E Fill in the blanks to show the morphographs in each word.

1. _____ + _____ = poisonous

2. _____ + _____ = famous

3. _____ + _____ = relate

4. _____ + _____ + _____ = relative

5. _____ + _____ + _____ = reaction

6. _____ + _____ + _____ = expression

END OF LESSON 108

Name _____

109

A

duty   danger   round   speak   fury   seize

B

1. _____
   _____

2. _____
   _____

C

1. _____   4. _____
2. _____   5. _____
3. _____

D Each sentence has one misspelled word. Write each word correctly on the blank.

1. Who knows whether the whether will change soon.   _____

2. The riseing water caused damage and defaced the land.   _____

3. She explained her plan for bringing about peace and reform.   _____

Lesson 109

E Write s or es in the second column. Then add the morphographs together.

                        s or es

1. tax + _____ = _____
2. brush + _____ = _____
3. claim + _____ = _____
4. waltz + _____ = _____
5. pass + _____ = _____
6. light + _____ = _____
7. reach + _____ = _____
8. rich + _____ = _____

F Add the morphographs together.

1. deny + al = _____
2. glory + ous = _____
3. press + ure = _____
4. mis + con + cept + ion = _____
5. un + ex + cept + ed = _____
6. flaw + ed = _____
7. thirst + y = _____
8. ex + press + ion = _____
9. in + ject + ion = _____
10. seize + ure = _____

Lesson 110 is a test lesson. There is no worksheet.

Name _____ 111

A

1. _____ 4. _____
2. _____ 5. _____
3. _____

B

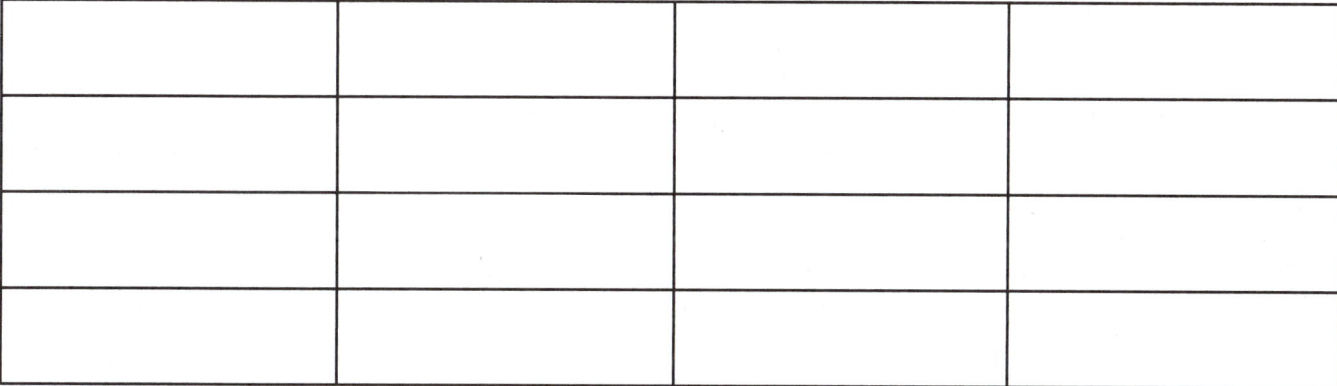

C Make 9 real words from the morphographs in the box.

| est | mad | happy | ly | wide | ness | fine |

1. _____ 6. _____
2. _____ 7. _____
3. _____ 8. _____
4. _____ 9. _____
5. _____

Lesson 111

D Fill in the blanks to show the morphographs in each word.

1. _____ + _____ + _____ = protective
2. _____ + _____ + _____ = injected
3. _____ + _____ + _____ = progressed
4. _____ + _____ + _____ = reception
5. _____ + _____ = texture
6. _____ + _____ + _____ = featuring
7. _____ + _____ = passion
8. _____ + _____ = studying
9. _____ + _____ = studious
10. _____ + _____ = signal

E Each sentence has one misspelled word. Write each word correctly on the blank.

1. They were surprised by the gloryous cities they discovered. _____

2. They expressed delight over the unexpected outcome. _____

3. Everybody who was on duty felt frightened and edgey. _____

END OF LESSON 111

182   Lesson 111

Name _____ 112

A

The union of physical science and logic was a major development.

_____

_____

B   **s** or **es**

1. worry + _____ = _____

2. play + _____ = _____

3. try + _____ = _____

4. joy + _____ = _____

5. copy + _____ = _____

6. boy + _____ = _____

7. story + _____ = _____

8. study + _____ = _____

9. stay + _____ = _____

10. duty + _____ = _____

C

1. _____ 4. _____

2. _____ 5. _____

3. _____

D
Add the morphographs together.
Remember to use your spelling rules.

1. danger + ous = _____
2. seize + ure = _____
3. fury + ous = _____
4. script + ure = _____
5. quest + ion + able = _____
6. poison + ous = _____
7. fur + y = _____
8. please + ure = _____
9. friend + ly + ness = _____
10. re + fuse + al = _____

E
Cross out the misspelled words in these sentences.
Then write the words correctly above the crossed-out words.

Could you speak a little lowder, please?

Where are the fameous people?

Their was no reeson for the rejection.

END OF LESSON 112

Name _____ **113**

A

___ __i o__ __

__y s_____ ___e_c_

___ _o g__ ___ _

__j o_ ___e_o_____.

_____

_____

B

1. _____ 5. _____
2. _____ 6. _____
3. _____ 7. _____
4. _____ 8. _____

C   s or es

1. boy + _____ = _____
2. story + _____ = _____
3. try + _____ = _____
4. worry + _____ = _____
5. baby + _____ = _____
6. fly + _____ = _____
7. berry + _____ = _____
8. carry + _____ = _____

D

1. _____ 4. _____
2. _____ 5. _____
3. _____

E These words are in the word search. Circle 7 or more of the words.

poison   found
pound   concept
lone   pity
store   fact
photo   whose
flat   proven

```
p  p  w  h  o  s  e  f
p  o  i  s  o  n  s  p
c  o  n  c  e  p  t  r
f  o  u  n  d  h  o  o
a  l  o  n  e  o  r  v
c  p  a  r  d  t  e  e
t  p  i  t  y  o  e  n
```

END OF LESSON 113

Name _____ 114

A

— — — — — — — — — —

— — — — — — — — — — — — — —

— — — — — — — — — — — —

— — — — — — — — — — — — — — — .

_____

_____

B

1. _____

2. _____

C

1. _____ 4. _____

2. _____ 5. _____

3. _____ 6. _____

Lesson 114 **187**

D Write s or es in the second column.
Then add the morphographs together.

1. worry + _____ = _____
2. pinch + _____ = _____
3. truck + _____ = _____
4. story + _____ = _____
5. copy + _____ = _____
6. poison + _____ = _____
7. study + _____ = _____
8. cry + _____ = _____

E Complete each sentence correctly with these words:

| whole | write | hole | features |
| varies | right | weather | morning |

1. Caron's experiment failed, but she had the _____ idea.
2. Tony is going to _____ a short story.
3. Our boat won't float because it has a large _____ in it.
4. I can't eat a _____ cake.
5. Murphy's Cafe _____ fried chicken every Friday.
6. Robin exercises every _____ .
7. The _____ in Trinidad rarely _____ .
8. Tahiti _____ great _____ .

This is the last worksheet in Grade 3.
There are no worksheets for Lessons 115–120.

Word List

WORD **LESSON**

Word	Lesson
a	21
above	52
act	41
action	88
active	84
actively	90
agree	104
all	119
am	63
an	14
answer	7
answers	67
anybody	106
are	59
aren't	58
arms	24
asked	116
at	94
athlete	71
athletes	96
author	6
authoring	11
babies	82
baby	42
babyish	59
backs	24
bar	37
bare	37
bared	24
baring	24
barred	54
base	45
basement	51
be	51
beautiful	77
beautifully	83
beauty	73
before	71
believe	44
bench	12
benches	32
berries	113
berry	17
best	22
big	46
biggest	12
blackness	87
bliss	47
blissful	12
bloomed	46
blow	39
blowing	53
boat	22
boats	26
boldness	6
book	56
box	28
boxes	32
boxing	32
boy	17
boyish	56
boyishness	8
boys	68
brain	51
break	6
breakable	39
breath	93
breathe	57
breathing	94
bridge	101
brief	77
briefest	81
briefly	79
brother	37
brotherly	67
brown	67
brownish	16
brush	48
brushes	27
build	1
building	1
bush	49
bushes	29
busiest	64
business	62
busy	11
busyness	62
buzz	37
buzzes	107
by	62
can	104
can't	56
care	3
cared	24
careful	26
carefully	21
careless	3
carelessly	18
carriage	96
carried	29
carrier	56
carries	82
carry	18
carrying	38
catch	22
catches	28
caught	7
cause	47
cent	50
chain	51
chalk	12
change	33
changes	69
changing	33
charge	9
charging	9
charm	52
cheap	2
cheapest	2
chief	77
chiefly	81
child	3
childish	18
childishly	21
childishness	74
childless	3
children	32
choice	1
choicest	54
choke	51
choking	6
chop	52
choppy	17
cities	86
city	53
civil	33
civilly	33
claim	32
claims	32
clapping	42
class	54
classes	28
close	13
clothes	12
cloud	3
clouded	8
cloudiest	53
cloudiness	46

Word List

WORD			LESSON
cloudless	1	copied	26
clouds	66	copier	24
cloudy	17	copies	82
coat	22	copy	24
coats	27	copying	25
coin	42	could	42
cold	42	couldn't	57
coldly	11	count	64
come	56	counting	71
coming	66	countless	86
concept	106	cover	73
confine	33	crashes	28
confined	57	crease	101
confinement	49	create	104
confining	41	creative	104
confirmed	42	cried	61
conform	29	crier	28
conformed	72	cries	82
conforming	31	cry	28
confront	29	crying	34
confronted	71	curable	7
confuse	42	cure	46
confused	51	danger	73
confusing	41	dangerous	94
conjecture	108	dark	58
conquest	94	darken	12
consent	48	darkness	6
conserve	39	date	27
consign	29	day	102
consignment	54	deal	59
constrict	31	dealer	26
constricted	38	deception	112
contacted	77	deceptive	106
contain	114	defacing	63
contest	43	defeat	61
context	42	defeated	71
contract	42	define	11
contracted	54	defined	11
contraction	96	defining	35

WORD			LESSON
dejected	108	disease	28
delight	11	dish	28
delighted	27	dishes	28
delightful	3	does	56
denial	31	doesn't	58
denied	26	door	14
dented	41	dosage	42
deny	26	dose	42
denying	63	doubt	93
depart	11	doubtful	116
departed	12	doubtfully	96
department	49	doubtless	94
deport	19	drag	12
deported	43	dragging	12
depressed	39	drain	51
depressing	33	drainage	57
depression	92	dress	18
describe	113	dresses	29
deserve	33	dressy	18
deserved	21	dried	28
design	26	drink	33
designed	36	drip	16
designer	21	dripped	16
desk	48	dripping	51
desks	41	drive	103
detain	114	driving	103
detect	107	drop	14
detecting	106	dropped	98
detection	112	dropper	14
detective	107	dropping	28
detract	51	dry	28
development	112	drying	30
did	24	dull	63
didn't	58	duties	112
different	13	duty	109
dine	56	earlier	53
dined	24	earliest	49
diner	24	early	46
dining	24	ease	28

Word List

WORD				LESSON
easily	39	farming	16	flawed	107	frost	18

WORD	LESSON
easily	39
easy	27
edge	107
edgy	107
eight	46
else	71
enough	57
equal	2
equally	22
error	46
especially	82
everyone	71
except	107
exception	113
exchange	62
exchanging	77
exciting	82
exclaim	66
exercise	106
exercised	96
explain	85
explained	68
export	62
exported	67
exports	89
express	62
expressed	107
expression	93
expressive	88
fact	113
fail	34
fair	94
fame	108
famous	94
fanciest	29
fanciful	27
fancy	18
farm	9
farmer	9
farming	16
farms	29
fashion	94
fashionable	96
fatally	42
fate	42
fault	22
faultless	3
feat	4
feature	106
features	114
featuring	111
feel	41
feet	6
fell	79
fight	6
fighter	29
final	14
finally	27
fine	6
finely	16
finest	6
finish	81
finished	71
fire	22
fired	22
fires	94
firm	42
first	79
fish	69
fit	12
fitness	12
fitting	91
flame	41
flat	9
flatly	14
flatten	42
flattest	31
flaw	108
flawed	107
flier	56
flies	83
float	22
floated	54
floating	42
flop	12
flopping	12
flow	39
flower	54
flowers	46
fluid	42
fly	22
flying	41
fool	16
foolish	16
foolishly	38
for	59
force	37
forceful	54
forcefully	37
form	14
formal	14
formally	26
former	72
formless	29
forms	28
found	42
fox	28
foxes	33
freshen	12
friend	29
friendliest	63
friendliness	29
friendly	42
friends	24
fright	99
from	81
front	37
frost	18
frosty	18
fudge	24
funny	21
fur	18
furious	27
furry	18
fury	109
fuse	41
gain	51
girl	33
girlishness	33
glass	28
glasses	28
global	19
globe	19
glories	86
glorious	97
glory	4
goat	22
goats	27
going	68
gold	27
golden	19
gone	56
good	59
govern	79
government	83
grab	16
grabbed	16
grace	22
graceful	22
gracefully	29
great	114
greatest	62
greatness	53
grief	77
grip	77
gripped	118

Word List **191**

Word List

WORD			LESSON
gripping 77	he's 54	injected 111	leader 44
ground 69	him 43	injection 108	leak 41
grow 39	hired 57	inland 28	leakage 41
grudge 9	his 94	inside 33	leakages 71
guide 93	hit 22	instated 42	leave 32
gum 17	hole 17	instead 106	length 18
gummy 17	hope 7	instilled 41	lengthen 51
had 28	hoped 44	insure 42	lengthening 47
happier 24	hopeful 24	intake 28	lengthy 23
happiest 32	hopefully 26	intended 58	let's 59
happily 33	hopeless 7	intensive 99	light 2
happiness 26	hopelessly 11	interested 101	lighten 12
happy 2	hopelessness 14	into 117	lighter 64
hard 57	hoping 13	invaluable 37	lightest 2
hardened 99	hot 22	investment 52	lighting 2
harm 27	hotly 33	investments 53	lightly 11
harmless 118	hotter 86	is 32	lights 27
harmlessly 27	hottest 66	isn't 57	likable 7
hasn't 54	house 43	it 32	like 6
hate 22	huge 64	it's 54	likeliest 29
have 102	human 24	I've 56	likeliness 33
haven't 59	humans 24	joy 22	likely 41
he 38	hurried 26	joyful 59	likeness 6
headed 94	hurries 103	joyfully 64	likes 102
healthy 106	hurry 23	joyous 24	listen 1
hear 8	hurrying 39	joys 82	listened 8
heard 22	I 28	judge 22	listening 1
heaviest 69	if 118	jumpy 17	load 57
heavy 57	I'll 61	kindness 43	loan 36
he'll 57	in 101	know 24	lock 4
help 8	inactive 90	lake 81	locked 14
helped 8	income 66	landed 66	logic 112
helpful 2	incurable 37	large 8	lone 32
helpfully 14	inflaming 41	largely 64	loneliest 63
helpless 120	inform 28	largest 8	loneliness 41
helplessly 62	informal 28	late 22	lonely 37
helplessness 8	informed 43	lately 22	long 83
her 22	informer 33	latest 59	longer 9
here 3	inhuman 31	law 88	loose 99

Word List

WORD		LESSON

Word	Lesson
loud	67
louder	112
loudest	68
loudly	66
lovable	9
love	9
low	39
lower	98
luck	31
luckily	53
lucky	31
lunch	29
lunches	29
mad	11
madden	46
madder	41
maddest	13
madly	11
madness	12
main	32
mainly	44
maintain	114
major	112
make	41
many	102
mark	27
mash	22
match	56
matches	27
me	38
meet	94
mess	29
messes	29
might	8
mighty	21
misconception	109
misjudge	22
misplaced	39
misprinted	58
misquote	4
misquoted	21
misshaped	11
misspell	4
misspelled	82
misspelling	19
mistake	4
mistaken	27
misuse	27
morning	96
mother	54
mothering	54
motoring	31
motors	28
movable	64
move	32
movement	49
mover	66
moving	42
nail	34
nails	38
name	93
namely	96
nastier	86
nastiest	86
nastily	86
neat	32
neatly	33
neatness	91
nerve	32
nervous	103
nice	9
nicely	29
nicer	9
niece	77
night	94
nightly	77
nights	29
nineteen	96
noise	11
noisiness	68
noisy	19
norm	16
normal	16
normally	33
not	24
notable	14
note	13
noted	98
notion	96
nudge	71
nudging	71
of	42
off	79
often	69
on	34
one	71
other	81
our	46
pack	13
package	13
packages	102
packaging	61
paint	8
painted	53
painter	37
paints	34
part	12
parts	24
pass	109
passage	13
passes	27
passion	107
passive	84
patch	34
patches	34
pause	47
pay	23
payment	49
peace	71
peaceful	71
peacefully	77
people	4
person	12
personal	19
personally	46
photo	113
photograph	101
physical	112
picture	7
pictures	34
piece	74
pills	24
pinch	14
pinches	29
pitied	33
pitiful	24
pity	21
pitying	46
place	12
placement	49
plain	47
plan	17
plane	48
planned	33
planner	31
planners	36
planning	17
plans	103
plants	29
play	17
played	44
player	26
playful	24
playfully	47
playing	79
plays	82

Word List **193**

Word List

WORD			LESSON
please 7	progress 106	quiz 68	refreshing 120
pleasing 24	progressed 106	quotable 11	refreshment 51
pleasure 112	progression 107	quote 2	refreshments 71
point 58	progressive 109	quoting 6	refusal 112
pointless 39	project 108	race 43	regained 68
points 28	projecting 112	races 43	regress 107
poison 47	projection 114	racing 31	regressing 106
poisoning 76	prolong 82	rage 59	reinform 72
poisonous 97	prolonged 83	raging 59	reinformed 72
poisons 114	proportion 104	rail 36	reinstate 31
port 6	protect 107	rain 33	reject 108
portable 7	protection 107	rainy 17	rejecting 107
pound 113	protective 111	rather 106	rejection 109
power 93	proud 67	ration 104	relate 49
powerful 94	proudly 106	reach 32	related 23
predated 27	prove 13	reaches 32	relation 93
preplanned 33	proven 24	react 64	relative 84
preschool 43	proverb 88	reacting 41	relatively 101
present 9	proving 21	reaction 88	remain 37
presented 18	provision 99	read 41	remaining 38
preserve 43	prowl 67	real 22	remark 7
preserved 19	pup 18	really 22	remarkable 7
preserving 9	puppy 18	reason 79	removal 42
press 28	pure 13	reasonable 83	remove 71
presses 28	purely 21	reasons 89	removed 56
pressure 106	purest 13	rebuild 1	removing 56
preview 9	quest 68	rebuilding 6	rent 16
previewed 27	question 7	recently 66	rental 14
prewash 9	questionable 51	reception 107	rented 24
prewrap 59	questions 26	receptive 106	renter 24
price 93	quick 68	recover 79	renting 24
print 58	quickest 86	refine 38	repack 1
probe 96	quickly 73	refined 14	repainted 8
probing 96	quiet 6	refinement 56	replace 43
proclaim 82	quieter 9	reformed 16	replaced 12
proclaimed 104	quietest 7	reformer 72	replacement 71
profile 82	quietly 11	refresh 74	replacing 91
profound 96	quietness 6	refreshed 19	report 67
profoundly 83	quite 69	refreshes 74	reported 64

Word List

WORD		LESSON
reporter		27
repression		88
repressive		106
request		71
requesting		76
research		1
researcher		21
researches		74
reservation		52
reserve		19
reserved		37
reserving		63
resign		33
resigned		54
resolve		96
resort		36
resource		3
resourceful		14
resources		74
rest		22
restful		26
restfully		26
restless		26
restlessly		26
restlessness		23
restore		96
restricted		77
retain		114
retract		43
review		1
rewrap		90
rich		94
riches		108
right		2
rightful		98
rightfully		61
ring		1
ripe		6
ripeness		7
ripest		6
rise		66
risen		8
rising		66
robber		56
room		81
roominess		99
rooms		26
rose		17
rosy		17
roughest		64
round		69
ruin		42
ruined		46
run		11
runner		11
running		12
runny		107
sack		22
sad		9
sadden		14
saddening		64
sadder		63
saddest		11
sadly		11
sadness		16
safe		21
safely		21
safest		54
sail		22
sailboat		11
sailboats		81
sailing		59
sale		51
saw		14
school		6
schools		27
science		112
scratch		29
scratched		64
scratches		49
scribe		99
script		101
scripts		108
scripture		112
search		1
searched		1
searching		1
second		82
seize		109
seizure		109
self		17
selfish		16
selfishly		17
selfishness		18
sent		48
serve		9
served		24
server		24
serving		11
settle		104
several		12
shape		11
shaping		120
she		21
she'll		58
she's		57
shine		8
shining		8
shiny		17
ship		58
shipment		58
shop		22
shopper		17
shopping		24
shops		24
short		38
should		33
shouldn't		54
show		39
shrink		101
sick		31
side		33
sign		2
signal		37
signs		24
skate		18
skating		21
sketch		11
skid		97
skidded		97
skipping		8
slam		41
slammed		41
sleep		2
sleeping		1
sleepless		3
sleeplessness		7
sleepy		17
slice		52
slightly		77
slip		107
slipping		92
slow		42
smile		62
snail		34
snap		37
snapped		107
snapping		104
snug		9
snugness		42
solve		94
some		21
sore		6
soreness		6
sort		1
sorted		8

Word List

WORD			LESSON
sound 57	statements 104	stretcher 104	tell 22
soundly 63	station 88	stretches 28	tend 58
soundness 66	stay 22	stretching 3	tense 101
sounds 68	stayed 26	strict 31	tension 99
source 3	stays 82	stuck 43	test 63
sources 53	step 22	studied 26	text 42
south 67	stepped 95	studies 82	texture 106
speak 14	stepping 21	studious 104	that 34
speaker 16	still 41	study 4	that's 71
speech 33	stitch 31	studying 29	the 7
speeches 27	stitches 31	sturdier 26	their 63
speed 58	stone 18	sturdiest 28	them 93
speediest 58	stony 18	sturdily 86	there 81
speedy 106	stop 11	sturdiness 27	they 93
spell 3	stopped 11	sturdy 17	they'd 88
spelling 3	stopping 13	style 8	they'll 59
spin 14	storage 17	styled 9	they're 56
spinning 14	store 17	stylish 21	they've 93
spirit 104	stored 41	stylishly 41	thickness 43
sport 120	stories 82	sudden 73	thief 77
spot 13	storing 97	suddenly 77	thirst 104
spotless 21	story 8	sunny 19	thirsty 109
spotted 13	straight 2	sure 57	this 24
sprain 51	straighten 12	surprise 82	those 59
spray 23	straighter 11	surprised 94	thought 8
sprayed 32	straightest 2	swim 11	thoughtful 12
sprays 83	strained 58	swimmer 17	thoughtfully 92
stage 6	strange 47	swimming 11	thoughtfulness 18
staged 17	strangely 48	tact 77	thoughtless 43
staging 6	strangeness 51	tail 29	thoughtlessly 12
stain 51	stranger 49	tails 29	thoughtlessness 8
stained 51	strangest 49	take 8	thoughts 89
star 12	strength 18	taken 54	threw 46
starred 12	strengthen 19	tale 101	throat 22
starring 14	strengthening 33	talked 98	through 12
stars 29	stress 94	tax 28	throughout 96
state 21	stretch 3	taxes 32	throw 39
stately 21	stretchable 7	teach 22	time 9
statement 49	stretched 8	teacher 22	timeless 9

196 Word List

Word List

WORD			LESSON
times 102	type 79	untyped 83	wasn't 54
to 24	unarmed 36	unvaried 58	watch 41
together 7	unbreakable 7	unwashable 8	watched 93
tone 101	uncivilly 59	unwrap 13	watches 46
too 108	unclaimed 33	usable 8	watching 84
took 102	unclear 39	usage 19	water 12
touched 57	unconfirmed 52	use 8	watering 12
touching 52	uncovered 81	useful 26	we 22
tough 49	undefeated 42	useless 8	weather 39
toughest 49	undeserving 66	uselessly 26	week 102
town 69	undrinkable 33	using 104	we'll 61
toy 83	unending 17	valuable 19	were 62
toys 83	unequal 2	value 18	we're 56
trace 24	unequally 12	varied 31	weren't 58
tracing 86	uneven 2	varies 114	we've 56
tract 42	unexcepted 109	various 94	what 51
trail 34	unexplained 71	vary 21	what's 59
trailer 46	unfairly 99	verb 88	where 120
trap 59	unhappy 2	verbal 14	whether 43
trapped 64	uninformed 38	verbally 66	which 86
trapper 33	union 112	very 26	who 56
traps 67	unkindness 52	vest 52	whole 16
treat 101	unlikeliness 31	view 1	whose 32
treatment 106	unlikely 12	viewing 1	wide 11
trial 56	unlucky 41	voice 8	widely 11
tribal 17	unmistakable 54	volt 18	widest 12
tribe 17	unmoved 64	voltage 38	will 102
tricky 37	unneeded 16	wake 52	win 21
tried 31	unplanned 21	waltz 109	winner 21
tries 82	unpreserved 27	waltzes 109	winners 48
trip 22	unproven 14	wander 1	wire 18
tripped 97	unquotable 76	wandered 29	wiry 18
trips 29	unreadable 41	wandering 1	wishes 29
truck 114	unrecoverable 79	warm 18	won 99
trucks 114	unrefined 61	warmest 18	wonder 23
try 23	unrelated 61	was 56	wondered 51
trying 29	unsnapped 58	wash 8	wonderful 48
turn 32	unsound 64	washable 7	wonderfully 23
twice 11	unsturdy 63	washes 28	wondering 43

Word List **197**

Word List

WORD			LESSON
wood 79	worry 27	wrapped 98	yellow 17
woods 22	worrying 32	wrapper 13	you 17
work 68	worth 13	wrapping 56	you'll 54
world 9	worthiness 96	wreck 13	your 38
worldly 21	worthless 13	wreckage 13	you're 61
worlds 74	worthy 31	write 1	you've 58
worried 27	would 38	writing 8	
worrier 63	wouldn't 56	wrong 7	
worries 82	wrap 13	wrote 38	

Study Lists

1–5
build
building
care
cheap
cheapest
child
childless
cloud
cloudless
equal
glory
happy
light
lightest
lighting
listen
listening
lock
misquote
people
quote
rebuild
repack
research
resource
review
right
search
sign
sleep
sleepless
sort
source
spell
spelling
straight
straightest
stretch
stretching
study
unequal
uneven
unhappy
view
wander
wandering
write

6–10
answer
author
boldness
break
careless
caught
charge
charging
choice
choking
clouded
curable
darkness
farmer
fight
finest
grudge
helped
helplessness
hopeless
largest
likable
likeness
listened
longer
lovable
might
mistake
nicer
picture
please
port
portable
present
preserving
preview
prewash
question
quiet
quieter
quietest
quietness
quoting
rebuilding
remarkable
repainted
ripeness
ripest
school
searching
serve
shining
sleeping
sleeplessness
soreness
sorted
staging
story
stretchable
stretched
style
styled
thought
thoughtlessness
timeless
together
unbreakable
unending
unwashable
usable
useless
voice
washable
world
writing
wrong

11–15
authoring
bench
biggest
blissful
busy
chalk
coldly
darken
define
defined
delight
delightful
depart
departed
different
dragging
final
fitness
flopping
formal
freshen
helpful
helpfully
here
hopelessly
hopelessness
hoping
lighten
lightly
madly
madness
misshaped
noise
notable
note
package
passage
person
pinch
prove
pure
purest
quietly
quotable
refined
rental
replaced
resourceful
runner
running
saddest
sadly
sailboat
serving
several
sketch
speak
starred
stopped
straighter
swimming
thoughtful
thoughtlessly
through
twice
unequally

Study Lists

unlikely
unproven
verbal
watering
widely
widest
worthless
wreck
wreckage

16–20

brownish
carelessly
carry
childish
choppy
cloudy
dressy
dripped
fancy
farming
finely
foolish
frosty
furry
global
golden
grabbed
gummy
hole
jumpy
length
misspell
misspelling
noisy
normal
personal
planning
presented
preserved

puppy
rainy
reformed
refreshed
reserve
rosy
sadness
selfish
selfishly
selfishness
shiny
shopper
skate
sleepy
speaker
spinning
starring
stony
storable
straighten
strength
strengthen
sturdy
sunny
swimmer
thoughtfulness
tribal
unneeded
usage
valuable
value
warmest
whole
wiry
wrapper

21–25

bared
baring
biggest

cared
carefully
childishly
coat
copied
copying
deserved
designer
dined
diner
dining
equally
faultless
fired
float
fudge
funny
goat
graceful
hopeful
lately
lengthy
mighty
misjudge
nice
pitiful
playful
pleasing
proven
proving
purely
really
related
rented
renter
renting
researcher
restlessness
safely
sail

served
server
shopping
skating
spotless
stately
stepping
stylish
teacher
throat
trace
unplanned
vary
winner
wonderfully
worldly

26–30

arms
boats
box
brushes
bushes
careful
carried
catches
classes
coats
conform
confront
consign
crashes
crier
dealer
delighted
denied
design
disease
dishes
dresses

dried
dropping
drying
easy
fanciest
fanciful
farms
fighter
finally
formally
formless
forms
fox
friendliness
friends
glasses
goats
gracefully
happiness
harmlessly
hopefully
hurried
inform
informal
inland
intake
lights
likeliest
lunches
matches
messes
mistaken
motors
nicely
nights
pinches
plants
player
points
predated

Study Lists

presses
previewed
questions
reporter
restful
restfully
restless
restlessly
rooms
sadden
schools
scratch
shops
speeches
stars
stayed
stretches
studied
studying
sturdier
sturdiness
tails
tax
trips
trying
unpreserved
useful
uselessly
very
washes
wishes
worried

31–35

benches
boxes
boxing
changing
children
civilly
claim
claims
confine
conforming
constrict
crying
defining
degrade
denial
depressing
deserve
fail
foxes
girlishness
happiest
happily
hotly
informer
inhuman
inside
leave
likeliness
lone
lucky
maddest
main
motoring
move
nail
neat
neatly
normally
patches
pitied
planned
planner
preplanned
reaches
reinstate
resign
sick
signs
snail
sprayed
stitches
taxes
trail
trapper
tried
turn
unclaimed
undrinkable
unlikeliness
varied
whose
worrying
worthy

36–40

blow
breakable
carrying
conserve
depressed
easily
flow
foolishly
forcefully
grow
incurable
invaluable
know
loan
lonely
low
misplaced
nails
pointless
rail
refine
remain
remaining
reserved
show
sturdiest
throw
tricky
unclear
uninformed
voltage
weather

41–45

clapping
confining
confirmed
confusing
contest
context
contract
dosage
fatally
flatten
flattest
fluid
flying
hoped
inflaming
instated
instilled
leader
leakage
loneliness
moving
played
races
reacting
removal
retract
ruin
slammed
snugness
spray
stylishly
text
tract
undefeated
unlucky
unreadable
whether

46–50

bloomed
boyishness
cause
cloudiness
confinement
consent
darkness
department
earliest
early
flowers
informed
lengthening
madden
movement
our
pause
payment
personally
placement
plain
playfully
poison
relate
ruined
scratches
spotted
statement
strange
strangely
stranger
strangest
toughest

Study Lists

trailer
watches
winners
wonderful
yellow

51–55

barred
basement
choicest
cloudiest
consignment
contracted
detract
drain
earlier
forceful
gain
hasn't
he's
investment
investments
it's
luckily
mothering
questionable
rain
refreshment
resigned
safest
sale
shouldn't
signal
sources
sprain
stain
stained
strangeness
taken
unconfirmed
unmistakable

wasn't
you'll

56–60

aren't
babyish
boyish
breathe
can't
carrier
confined
couldn't
didn't
doesn't
drainage
flier
hard
haven't
heavy
he'll
intended
isn't
I've
joyful
latest
let's
light
load
make
misprinted
painter
prewrap
raging
refinement
removed
removing
rewrap
she'll
she's
shipment
speediest

strained
sure
they'll
they're
touched
trial
uncivilly
unsnapped
unvaried
we're
weren't
we've
what's
wouldn't
wrapping
you've

61–65

busiest
business
busyness
cried
defacing
denying
exchange
export
express
friendliest
greatest
helplessly
I'll
it's
let's
loneliest
packaging
remark
reserving
rightfully
saddening
sadder
scratched

she's
soundly
strengthening
their
unequally
unrefined
unrelated
unsturdy
we'll
worrier
you're

66–70

brown
count
exclaim
explained
exported
ground
heaviest
hottest
income
loudly
mainly
mover
noisiness
proud
prowl
quest
quick
quiz
recently
regained
rising
round
soundness
sounds
south
town
undeserving
verbally

71–75

athlete
beauty
before
conformed
confronted
counting
danger
defeated
else
everyone
finished
former
it's
let's
nudging
one
peace
racing
reformer
reinform
reinformed
replacement
request
sudden
that's
wondered

76–80

beautiful
brief
chief
contacted
exchanging
first
govern
grief
gripping
house
largely

Study Lists

niece
nightly
peaceful
peacefully
reason
requesting
restricted
roughest
slightly
suddenly
thief
type
unquotable
unrecoverable

81–85

active
babies
beautifully
boys
briefest
briefly
carries
chiefly
copies
cries
especially
exciting
explain
flies
government
joys
passive
plays
proclaim
profile
profoundly
prolong
prolonged
relative
second

sprays
stays
stories
studies
surprise
threw
toys
trapped
tries
uncovered
untyped
worries

86–90

action
actively
blackness
cities
expressive
glories
hotter
inactive
nastier
nastiest
nastily
proverb
react
reaction
reasonable
reasons
repression
station
sturdily
they'd
thoughts
watching

91–95

breath
conquest

dangerous
depression
doubt
doubtless
expression
fair
famous
fashion
fitting
globe
guide
joyous
name
neatness
power
powerful
price
relation
replace
rich
slipping
solve
stepped
they've
thoughtfully
thoughtless
tribe
various
what's

96–100

athletes
carriage
changes
contraction
derailed
doubtfully
dripping
dropped
exercised
fashionable

fright
glorious
hardened
intensive
joyfully
loose
morning
namely
nineteen
notion
poisoning
poisonous
probing
profound
provision
quickest
resolve
restore
rightful
roominess
scribe
short
skidded
store
tension
throughout
tough
tripped
unfairly
worthiness

101–105

agree
crease
creative
driving
furious
hurries
interested
nervous
photograph

plans
proclaimed
proportion
ration
relatively
script
settle
shrink
snapping
spirit
strict
studious
tense
thirst
tone
treat

106–110

anybody
buzzes
concept
conjecture
deceptive
deforming
dejected
detect
detecting
detective
duty
edgy
except
expressed
feature
flawed
fury
healthy
injection
instead
lower
misconception
passes

Study Lists

playing
poisoned
pressure
progress
progressed
progression
progressive
project
protect
protection
proudly
rather
reception
receptive

regress
regressing
reject
rejecting
rejection
repressive
rich
riches
runny
scripts
seize
seizure
snapped
speedy

texture
thirsty
treatment
unexcepted

111–115

berries
contain
deception
detain
detection
development
duties
exception

exercise
featuring
helpless
injected
logic
maintain
major
passion
physical
pleasure
poisons
preserve
projecting
projection

protective
retain
refreshing
science
scripture
shaping
sport
trucks
union
where

Spelling Rules

Lesson	Rule	Explanation
6	Final-E Rule	When do you drop the final **e** from a word? When the next morphograph begins with a vowel letter.
11	Doubling Rule	When do you double the final **c** in a short word? When the word ends **cvc** and the next morphograph begins with **v**.
17	Y as a Vowel	When is **y** a vowel letter? At the end of a morphograph.
24	Y-to-I Rule	When do you change the **y** to **i** in a word? When the word ends with a consonant-and-**y** and the next morphograph begins with anything except **i**.
27	E-S Endings	If a word ends in **s, sh,** or **ch**, you add **e-s** to make the plural word.
32	E-S Endings	If a word ends in **x**, you add **e-s** to make the plural word.
82	E-S Endings	If a word ends with a consonant-and-**y**, you add **e-s** to make the plural word.
88	W as a Vowel	When is **w** a vowel letter? At the end of a morphograph.
107	E-S Endings	If a word ends in **z**, you add **e-s** to make the plural word.

Meanings of Affixes and Nonword Bases

Morphograph	Lesson	Meanings	Examples
-able	7	can be	stretchable, washable, readable
-age	13	result of an action	package, usage, marriage
-al	14	related to, like	formal, trial, rental
cept	106	to take; contain	receptive, intercept, acceptable
con-	29	with, together	conform, contest, condense
de-	11	down, away from; reverse of; remove from	deport, deform, depart
-ed	8	(action) in the past	formed, stepped, cried
-en	12	to make	loosen, darken, straighten
-er	9	more; one who	greater, lighter; teacher, dancer
-es	27	more than one; a verb marker for *he, she,* or *it*	lilies, boxes; watches, catches
-est	2	the most	greatest, lightest, happiest
ex-	62	out, away	export, exclude, extend
-ful	12	full of; tending to	careful, beautiful; forgetful
gress	106	to step	regression, progress, transgression
in-	28	in, into; not; really	include; incurable; invaluable
-ing	1	when you do something, ongoing action	spending, moving, stopping
-ion	88	state, quality, act, or process	action, taxation, repression
-ish	16	like, related to, inclined to be	babyish, stylish, boyish, greenish

Meanings of Affixes and Nonword Bases

Morphograph	Lesson	Meanings	Examples
-ive	84	quality of; one who	expressive, informative; relative, detective
ject	107	to throw	rejecting, dejected, projection
-less	3	without	painless, useless, restless
-ly	11	how something is done	quietly, equally, basically
-ment	49	result of doing something	placement, requirement, apartment
mis-	4	wrongly	misspell, misjudge, misprint
-ness	6	that which is, quality of	quietness, freshness, thickness
-ous	94	having the quality of	famous, furious, joyous
pre-	9	before	preview, preclude, prepay
pro-	82	in favor of; before; forward	proclaim; provision; progress
re-	1	again, back	rerun, return, replace
-s	24	more than one; a verb marker for *he, she,* or *it*	friends, bananas, farmers; acts, writes, talks
tain	114	to hold	retaining, container, detained
tect	106	to cover	detecting, protection
un-	2	not, the opposite of	unhappy, unusual, untie
-ure	106	act, process	departure, pressure, failure
-y	17	having the quality of; belonging to	shiny, dreamy, mighty

Contractions

Component Words	Contractions	Component Words	Contractions
are not	aren't	she will	she'll
can not	can't	should not	shouldn't
could not	couldn't	they are	they're
did not	didn't	they had	they'd
does not	doesn't	they have	they've
has not	hasn't	they will	they'll
have not	haven't	was not	wasn't
he is	he's	we are	we're
he will	he'll	we will	we'll
I have	I've	were not	weren't
I will	I'll	what is	what's
is not	isn't	would not	wouldn't
it is	it's	you are	you're
let us	let's	you have	you've
she is	she's	you will	you'll

Homonyms

ate	refers to:	eat in the past
	example:	I *ate* a sandwich.
eight	refers to:	the number 8
	example:	The dog had *eight* puppies.
close	refers to:	shut something
	example:	Please *close* the door.
clothes	refers to:	things you wear
	example:	They bought lots of *clothes*.
feat	refers to:	something that is hard to do
	example:	Climbing the mountain was a great *feat*.
feet	refers to:	body parts
	example:	Her *feet* were sore from running.
for	refers to:	in place of
	example:	She went to the store *for* me.
four	refers to:	the number 4
	example:	Cats have *four* legs.
hear	refers to:	listen
	example:	I can't *hear* you.
here	refers to:	this place
	example:	Come over *here*.
hole	refers to:	empty space
	example:	I have a *hole* in my sock.
whole	refers to:	entire, complete
	example:	He ate the *whole* pie.
loan	refers to:	allow to borrow something
	example:	She will *loan* me lunch money.
lone	refers to:	by itself
	example:	There was a *lone* tree.
meat	refers to:	food from animals
	example:	Some people don't eat *meat*.
meet	refers to:	come together
	example:	We agreed to *meet* next week.
peace	refers to:	calm; no war
	example:	I like *peace* and quiet.
piece	refers to:	a part
	example:	I ate a *piece* of fruit.
plain	refers to:	simple; ordinary
	example:	She wore a *plain* black dress.
plane	refers to:	flat surface or air transportation
	example:	The *plane* landed safely.
right	refers to:	correct or opposite of left
	example:	All my answers were *right*. She wears a ring on her *right* hand.
write	refers to:	put words on paper
	example:	You must *write* neatly.

Homonyms

sail	refers to:	travel on water in a ship or a boat
	example:	We learned how to *sail* at camp.
sale	refers to:	available to buy or an offer at a cheaper price
	example:	Our house is for *sale*. He bought the shoes on *sale*.
tail	refers to:	the back end
	example:	The dog chased his *tail*.
tale	refers to:	a story
	example:	He told an interesting *tale*.
their	refers to:	belonging to them
	example:	It is *their* house.
there	refers to:	that place
	example:	Go over *there*.
they're	refers to:	they are
	example:	I think *they're* ready.
threw	refers to:	throw in the past
	example:	She *threw* the ball.
through	refers to:	in one side and out the other
	example:	We went *through* the tunnel.
vary	refers to:	change
	example:	His moods *vary* from day to day.
very	refers to:	really, quite, especially
	example:	That story is *very* imaginative.
wear	refers to:	have clothes on your body
	example:	What shall I *wear* today?
where	refers to:	what place
	example:	*Where* do you want to go?
weather	refers to:	what it feels like out of doors
	example:	Always wear a hat in cold *weather*.
whether	refers to:	if
	example:	I don't care *whether* I go or not.
wood	refers to:	what trees are made of
	example:	We need *wood* for the fire.
would	refers to:	what might happen
	example:	I *would* like to go to Paris.
your	refers to:	belonging to you
	example:	*Your* coat is blue.
you're	refers to:	you are
	example:	*You're* ready.

Test Charts

	Lesson 5	Lesson 10	Lesson 15	Lesson 20	Lesson 25	Lesson 30
Super Speller	25	25	25	25	25	25
	24	24	24	24	24	24
	23	23	23	23	23	23
Very Good Speller	22	22	22	22	22	22
	21	21	21	21	21	21
	20	20	20	20	20	20
	19	19	19	19	19	19
	18	18	18	18	18	18
	17	17	17	17	17	17
	16	16	16	16	16	16
	15	15	15	15	15	15
	14	14	14	14	14	14
	13	13	13	13	13	13
	12	12	12	12	12	12
	11	11	11	11	11	11
	10	10	10	10	10	10
	9	9	9	9	9	9
	8	8	8	8	8	8
	7	7	7	7	7	7
	6	6	6	6	6	6
	5	5	5	5	5	5
	4	4	4	4	4	4
	3	3	3	3	3	3
	2	2	2	2	2	2
	1	1	1	1	1	1

30-Lesson Total

138 = Super Speller

Test Charts

	Lesson 35	Lesson 40	Lesson 45	Lesson 50	Lesson 55	Lesson 60	30-Lesson Total
Super Speller	25	25	25	25	25	25	
	24	24	24	24	24	24	
	23	23	23	23	23	23	138 = Super Speller
Very Good Speller	22	22	22	22	22	22	
	21	21	21	21	21	21	
	20	20	20	20	20	20	
	19	19	19	19	19	19	
	18	18	18	18	18	18	
	17	17	17	17	17	17	
	16	16	16	16	16	16	
	15	15	15	15	15	15	
	14	14	14	14	14	14	
	13	13	13	13	13	13	
	12	12	12	12	12	12	
	11	11	11	11	11	11	
	10	10	10	10	10	10	
	9	9	9	9	9	9	
	8	8	8	8	8	8	
	7	7	7	7	7	7	
	6	6	6	6	6	6	
	5	5	5	5	5	5	
	4	4	4	4	4	4	
	3	3	3	3	3	3	
	2	2	2	2	2	2	
	1	1	1	1	1	1	

Test Charts

	Lesson 65	Lesson 70	Lesson 75	Lesson 80	Lesson 85	Lesson 90
Super Speller	25	25	25	25	25	25
	24	24	24	24	24	24
	23	23	23	23	23	23
Very Good Speller	22	22	22	22	22	22
	21	21	21	21	21	21
	20	20	20	20	20	20
	19	19	19	19	19	19
	18	18	18	18	18	18
	17	17	17	17	17	17
	16	16	16	16	16	16
	15	15	15	15	15	15
	14	14	14	14	14	14
	13	13	13	13	13	13
	12	12	12	12	12	12
	11	11	11	11	11	11
	10	10	10	10	10	10
	9	9	9	9	9	9
	8	8	8	8	8	8
	7	7	7	7	7	7
	6	6	6	6	6	6
	5	5	5	5	5	5
	4	4	4	4	4	4
	3	3	3	3	3	3
	2	2	2	2	2	2
	1	1	1	1	1	1

30-Lesson Total

138 = Super Speller

Test Charts

	Lesson 95	Lesson 100	Lesson 105	Lesson 110	Lesson 115	Lesson 120
Super Speller	25	25	25	25	25	25
	24	24	24	24	24	24
	23	23	23	23	23	23
Very Good Speller	22	22	22	22	22	22
	21	21	21	21	21	21
	20	20	20	20	20	20
	19	19	19	19	19	19
	18	18	18	18	18	18
	17	17	17	17	17	17
	16	16	16	16	16	16
	15	15	15	15	15	15
	14	14	14	14	14	14
	13	13	13	13	13	13
	12	12	12	12	12	12
	11	11	11	11	11	11
	10	10	10	10	10	10
	9	9	9	9	9	9
	8	8	8	8	8	8
	7	7	7	7	7	7
	6	6	6	6	6	6
	5	5	5	5	5	5
	4	4	4	4	4	4
	3	3	3	3	3	3
	2	2	2	2	2	2
	1	1	1	1	1	1

30-Lesson Total

138 = Super Speller